SOFT LANDINGS

SOFT LANDINGS

Spiritual Wisdom

Book One

Jerry McDaniel, Clairvoyant

Living Dreams Press
Living Dreams Press, Santa Barbara, CA

Printed in the United States of America

First Printing, July 2025

Published through Living Dreams Press, Santa Barbara, CA

ISBNs:
978-1-943951-43-7 (hardcover)
978-1-943951-42-0 (paperback)
978-0-9890941-9-1 (eBook)

Cover Design by Debra Lynne Katz

Table of Contents

DEDICATION

This book is dedicated to the memory of Carlos Medina, my heart and kidney donor to whom none of this would be possible.

May God bless all those who made the difficult decision to have their loved one's organs donated so that others may live.

Those of us that were the recipients owe you a debt that can never be repaid. God bless you and yours.

Carlos, thank you and your family for giving me a second chance.

I won't let you down.

ACKNOWLEDGEMENTS

Thanks to my wife Mary for saving my life.

Thanks to our daughter, Katie, for always being our little girl.

Thanks to our oldest son, Patrick, for always making us laugh.

Thanks to our youngest son, Andrew, for keeping us on our toes.

Thanks to Ashley for being a great daughter-in-law.

Thanks to Andrew (different Andrew) for being a great son-in-law.

Finally, our grandchildren, Quinn, Kellan, and Kelly.

Thank you for making our lives full of joy and happiness.

INTRODUCTION

For thirty-five years I had a career in sales and account management before I retired, and during that time I traveled extensively throughout the Southeastern United States. I was on the road 3-4 days a week, either driving or flying. When it came to flying, I've calculated that I've been on more than three hundred flights, and as anyone who has flown a lot knows, flying has its share of ups and downs: cancelled flights, rescheduled trips, mechanical or maintenance issues with the airplane, late arrivals and/or departures, and of course, the occasional close call.

Flying, on the other hand, does allow you to see parts of the country that you otherwise might not see. Beautiful cities lit up at night, lush hills and valleys, gorgeous bodies of water, magnificent mountains—the list is endless. However, there were also those landscapes that seemed to have within them a small town or two. When you're flying in a large airplane, small towns seem to whisk by in seconds. But small planes are still the only way to get to these small and remote places quickly.

Again, anyone who has flown for business or pleasure, especially on small planes, has likely experienced a few flights that didn't go as planned.

This could be because of the elements or any number of factors, such as a bird hitting the windshield. (I was on a flight like that.)

I remember one such flight that didn't go as planned. I was flying from Orlando to Tallahassee to see a chain of stores. Tallahassee is not a small town; it's the capital of Florida, but it's not a major metropolitan area. Back in the day when I was flying into Tallahassee, not many big jets were flying there, so you had to fly in a "puddle jumper." That slang should tell you how big the planes were. The distance from Orlando to Tallahassee is 250 miles by car, 218 miles by plane, so the flight is not a long one. Back to the flight, I'm sitting on this plane at night, and I can see out the window that the fog is extremely thick. I can also see the lights on the wings going on. off, and then on again. The gentleman sitting next to me said very casually and under his breath, "Great." I asked him what he meant. He says, "He's lost." I looked at him and said, almost in disbelief, "Lost? The pilot's lost?"

The gentleman said, "Yep. He's trying to find the river. Once he finds it, we should be ok." I sat back and prayed that the pilot would find the river that would lead us to the airport. I must mention that at this point, I learned through our conversation that this gentleman was a trainer for Apache helicopter pilots, which explains his calm demeanor while flying on a prop plane looking for a river at night.

We found the river and our path to the airport, in which we made a safe and soft landing. A soft landing is all we want and desire when we fly. Much like the river that the pilot was looking for and eventually found, life helps us navigate through the fog of trauma and pain so that we can find our own soft landings. Life gives us opportunities to be aware of when it comes to dealing with difficulties and to be mindful of finding soft landings so that we don't fall too deep, too long, and too hard. Sometimes we recognize these situations and where to go for help, even if it's strength from within that helps us cushion the fall so we can get up.

Sometimes, however, we don't recognize or know where help is or how to find it. This book will hopefully help you through that fog so that once you fall, you have the tools to help you get up again. Through common everyday words, phrases, and thoughts, the energy that Spirit has blessed this book with will help us all through the various fogs of turmoil in our lives. Perhaps look at this book as a map of fifty-five rivers that we can all locate to find some soft landings.

One last thing: once we find our soft-landing places, we have a responsibility to help others find theirs. It's time to assume the role of the Apache helicopter pilot who helped me calm down so that I knew we were going to land safely. Let's reassure others that we are there for them.

Peace

CHAPTER ONE

DISCOVERY

"There will always be serendipity involved in discovery."

—Jeff Bezos

OVERVIEW

Here's a definition of discovery: "The activity of seeing, finding, or gaining knowledge of something previously unknown." This describes our first chapter as we embark on a journey by looking at things differently, as we discover more about ourselves and the world we live in.

In this chapter we will explore subjects such as the most ingenious listening device ever created, a gift that is available to us all, the inner beauty of a tree, the simplicity of a domino, drumbeats, being aware of the Divine, and revisiting the person we used to be. Discovering more about ourselves is the only way to start this book. This chapter provides us all with opportunities for soft landings. Enjoy and know that we are all vessels designed to explore and discover.

Somebody is Listening

If we want to live a harmonious life, it makes sense that our mind, body, and spirit need to work together to obtain a proper balance. Think of a tripod; if one leg isn't doing its job by bearing the weight to maintain proper balance, then the tripod collapses. So it is with us; if our mind, body, and spirit are not working correctly, then our chance of living a harmonious and balanced life is in peril. When one of these aspects of ourselves is not working at full capacity, it can cause an imbalance in our overall essence, including our hopes and dreams and a full life.

Yes, somebody is listening. It's our body, and sometimes it doesn't know the difference between when we joke, using self-deprecating humor, and when we're telling the truth. It's a surprise to most when we're told that our body is an ingenious listening device.

The mind, body, and spirit (MBS) work together to create a pathway that goes to the divine. The MBS is constantly sending and receiving thousands if not millions of signals a day. The body is one of the most sophisticated listening devices ever created. When we're injured or sick or whenever our energy is drained, one of the first things we are told is "Listen to your body." Our emotions, feelings, words, thoughts, deeds, are all recorded by your mind, body, and spirit. There is no tricking this system. We cannot say one thing and then do the opposite and expect everything to work out well. Mainly because the MBS is not aligned.

If our body is healthy, but we say and think negative things, then mixed signals go to the body. If we think we are not worthy of love or respect, then these signals are sent to the body and the body acts accordingly. Soon this will translate into aches, pain, illnesses, mental instability, etc. Talking to ourselves even with humor (guilty as charged) serves no purpose because our body will take it seriously and react.

All of this happens because of the energy that is behind every thought, every word, every deed, and every action. The body, through signals of the mind and spirit, listens and translates at the same time. Could it be time for us to start using different languages to raise our vibration? Think about our words, thoughts, and actions if we are about to say, think, or do something that we know is wrong. We all have that feeling that we've done something wrong, no matter how we try to validate it. We often refer to it as our "guilty conscience." It's that and more. It's our MBS signaling to us that there is a reason why we feel guilty. It's because somebody is listening, and it is our body.

The Greatest Gift

It's often said that love is the greatest gift, but do we truly understand love? Love is a very strong emotion that carries with it the highest vibrations. Does love understand us? That appears to be a silly, non-whimsical question, but if we separate love from the other emotions and feelings and treat love as a separate entity, it is a question worth asking.

Love will find a way to us so that its purpose and mission of making our life fulfilling and worth living for is realized. To accommodate love in our lives we must be able to receive it. How do we receive love? Getting back to the mind, body, and spirit, listening to everything that we do. It's vital that we acknowledge the fact that we are loved, that we love others—some unconditionally—and that we demonstrate love in ordinary, normal ways in our everyday lives. How do we do that?

- Help those who don't ask for it.
- Help those who we think don't deserve it.
- Reach out to the people we love just to see how they are doing.
- Have a short memory of those that have hurt us.
- Have a long memory of those that we have hurt.
- Help those who do need it because that's what friends do.
- Do three random acts of kindness a day, one each for the mind, body, and spirit.

The best random acts of kindness are the ones that barely anybody notices but radiate in the Universe. Let's take just a few moments to close our eyes and send positive energy for situations that we know are troubling. Imagine a white light full of forgiveness or any other positive emotion you want, wrapped in love. Stretch out your hands, symbolically or literally, and send it to whoever you want. Call it prayer, meditation, or whatever you want to call it, but this is the power of sending love's energy. As a reminder, we need to take stock of our energy so that we don't get trapped in negative situations. Just by reaching out in a positive manner, we will raise the vibrations.

However, reaching out may not be enough to help people on a brighter and better path. When it comes to love, it's easy to be skeptical about all the above. Here are some statements about love that we have heard over the years, along with a response from a skeptic.

The greatest of these is love.

Skeptics response: "What about when I have felt abandoned and metaphorically left for dead? Love doesn't seem so great when I'm down on my luck."

Universe's response: "Instead of shooting off a flare for help, there are people around us waiting and wanting to help; we just have to be ready to receive it by asking for it."

Love unconditionally.

Skeptics response: “Really? When did that happen to me? Why should I waste my energy? Shouldn’t I expect the same in return?”

Universe’s response: “We get what we give. It’s the law of EEE. The Equal Exchange of Energy. At one point in our lives, we loved someone unconditionally. It’s time we learn to love unconditionally again.”

Love one another.

Skeptics response: “Don’t I deserve the same?”

Universe’s response: “We need to have awareness in our lives to recognize when someone or somebody loves us. We experience this multiple times a day, but we need to recognize it, even if it’s just a random act of kindness, which is done out of love. We do this by being aware of the love around us.”

Love is the answer.

Skeptics response: “To everything? I have a ton of questions in which love doesn’t seem to be the answer.

Universe’s response: “There’s no higher vibration in the Universe than love. Love might not be the answer to everything, but it can put us on the right path—or, at least, show us the path to a better and more fulfilling life. You have the answers within you.”

All you need is love.

Skeptics response: "I need more than that. This seems simple enough, but to me this is a pie in the sky type of statement. I'm not buying it."

Universe's response: "Nobody is selling anything but the chance to connect, feel the warmth, and sense the energy of other like-minded souls."

Love is diversity without the label.

Skeptics response: "I'm tired of having diversity shoved down my throat. I see diversity as disruptive, nothing more."

Universe's response: "Everything around us, including our homes, cars, places of worship, stores we frequent, schools our family members attend, places of workplaces, hospitals, and clinics… everything has the fingerprints and diverse DNA of people who have designed and physically built the structures, did the wiring, plumbing, and painting, crafted parts and appliances, made the chairs we sit on, prepared our food, drove the trucks that deliver our products to us or the stores, administered us shots when we were sick, performed operations on us, and used the instruments made for surgeons and nurses to save our lives.

The list of people who have improved our lives through their diverse love is endless. We're talking black people, brown people, white people, yellow people, and so on. I'm stopping here because there are more than 100 different skin tones in the world. There are also over 4,000 different religions in the world, so accept it or not, diversity makes our lives more peaceful, fulfilled, joyful, restful—you get the picture. We must enjoy the fruits of diversity's labor of love.

The Universe speaks the diverse languages of the divine.

What we're talking about is finding our self-love. Love thyself. With self-love, we can appreciate the fact that we are one in a billion (or 6 billion) and there's nobody like us. The creator doesn't have a cloning machine. We must invite love into our lives so that during those times when we feel alone, isolated, or abandoned, we can turn to our inner self and acknowledge that we are one of a kind and worthy of love.

It's great to receive love from others, it's what makes us whole in some ways, but we must embrace love first because that's what makes our soul leap with joy.

If we receive nothing in return, then that's ok because love doesn't operate in a checklist bubble.

We must invite love into our heart and soul.

Love is there for the taking, but we must ask for it with sincerity and desire in our heart.

Let's also not forget that our ancestors and loved ones who have passed are here to remind us of the fact that we are loved by many beyond the physical realm. Our loved ones who have passed never leave us, even though their physical presence is no longer with us. When we have felt that no one has shown us love, that we have been isolated, or when we have questions but no answers, we ask, “Where was love?”

Love was there in those times, but we may not have recognized it because love has many shapes and forms. Even as we breathe, the energy of love is present. Self-love is what the Universe wants for everyone. Love, especially self-love, transcends all thoughts, ideologies, good and bad works, and labels; the list is endless.

Love belongs to us all, starting with ourselves. Take a couple of minutes and think about the positive things in life that you’ve done and that you’re going to do. It will be difficult to navigate through the negative things in our lives because our thoughts are overwhelmingly negative. We can do this if we get through the “yes, but” phase of reflecting upon our good actions. “Did you do some beneficial things in life?” “Why yes, but...” If we can just learn to accept that we have performed good deeds, said healing, thoughtful words, and done nice things for people, and that we did these actions with love in our hearts, then we will recognize that sometimes love does require an invitation. I think we’ve all heard of the broken or lonely heart. Could it be time to simply say or think, “I need love in my heart, my life”? Inviting love into our lives is the greatest gift we could give to an aching heart. Sharing that same love with others is the second greatest gift.

The Tree of Burdens

Trees are symbolically and literally sacred temples to this world and the spirit realm. For centuries, trees have been known to represent life's growth, wisdom, prosperity, and even poetry and religion. They have also been known as symbols of strength, individuality, and expression, and the one symbol that has everyone talking—the interconnectedness of everything.

Science has proven that trees have a memory and, through their trunks, can communicate throughout the forest. With all this knowledge, both spiritual and scientific, why can't we go to our trees and unload our burdens?

Yes, it's going to look strange if we're somewhere talking to a tree or hugging a tree. But why not give it a shot? In my last book, *Beyond the Rational Realm, Lifting the Veil of the Spirit World*, I refer to trees as nature's cell towers. Trees communicate with each other; in Celtic folklore, trees are looked at as pathways or passages to the heavens with their branches reaching up and to the underworld with their roots running underground. What calls us to look at the beauty and symbolic significance of trees?

Sometimes, when we are depressed and feeling miserable, let's send our thoughts to the tree. The tree is strong and can take anything we throw at it. They are waiting for us to unload our burdens. Take a piece of paper, write down all the negative things that are happening in your life, and then find a safe place to burn it. Put ashes on the ground in front of a tree. Give that tree thanks for unburdening you of the heaviness that we all carry from time to time.

Just when we thought we did not have anyone who would listen, there is healing nearby that is willing and standing by to help us in our time of need.

A Domino Falls

One of the more fascinating sights I have seen, and I'm sure I'm not alone, is when someone sets up an elaborate display of hundreds if not thousands of dominoes. These displays can sometimes stretch out over couches, chairs, tables, kids' toys, make-shift bridges, tunnels, and towns. They can go up and down, in and out different rooms, and even descend to start another set of dominoes.

Some dominoes are noisy, then get quiet, then noisy again, all the while going from the traditional black and white to various colors and so on. The process begins with pushing a single domino to fall, with the hope that it will culminate in success as all the dominos fall consecutively, one after another, until they have all fallen. It may only take ninety seconds or so to watch the spectacle unfold, but we know that it took hours and hours to set it up perfectly.

When we look at how other people live their lives, seemingly in perfect harmony, we feel a sense of loss. We've all felt it.

We all know someone who has the perfect life, well-behaved children (while ours are climbing into the produce section at the grocery store), an amazing job and career, a great house, and so on. We get jealous because on the surface they have it all. It's as if all the dominoes in their lives have fallen perfectly and in an orderly fashion, never failing to knock down the next one in a perfect sequence.

That, however, is never the case.

The seemingly perfect people or situations we observe aren't perfect at all. They're just like us in that even though the dominoes have been placed in the perfect spots and ready for us to push the first one over, something always happens.

The dominos of others have pain, trauma, loss, addiction, and tragedy written all over them.

We could say that we're all in this together, but many people find that statement questionable. Let's just say that we share the same emotions, feelings, and experiences that others share.

Our well-thought-out and perfectly laid-out plans for ourselves and our family do not necessarily line up with God's plans, the Universe's plan, life's plan, and most importantly, the soul plan given to us on the day of our birth.

There is synchronicity in everything, but it might not be the time for our synchronicity.

We cannot see the curve balls of our plan coming our way, much less somebody else's plan. We are unable to see the struggles, pain, heartaches, and misery that others have endured as they try and try to align their life's dominoes every morning, only to watch them all fall at once or not at all.

We want to see our children do well, so we line up the education and career dominoes only to see mindsets change as they embark on different paths.

We then line up the relationship dominoes for us, only to see them fall time and time again.

Life dominoes will always change our plans, and that is a beautiful thing. Life dominoes will get in our way sometimes as a reminder that a higher power is at work and better days are ahead. When it comes to life in general, there are three major areas that drive our passion: health, relationships, and finances. The question is, are we where we expected to be in these areas five years ago? Ten years ago?

Take a piece of paper and divide it into three columns. Label the columns: health, relationships, and finance. Let us take a moment to see if we are where we expected to be five or ten years ago. If we are, that's great; congratulations to us. But if we're not, let's write down underneath the headings reasons (not excuses) to see what happened. This little exercise requires honesty and transparency in order to be somewhat eye-opening. Reflecting upon this, a question pops up that needs our attention. Could it be time for us to set up a new set of dominoes that will create a new path towards a new life? It all starts with a single domino falling. The rest is up to us.

Drumbeat of Fear

Depending on who you listen to or read, there are six basic human emotions: sadness, happiness, anger, disgust, surprise, and fear. This is an updated list, as contempt used to be the seventh emotion, but somewhere along the way, it got dropped.

From these basic emotions, spring forth multiple emotional spinoffs that give energy to the basic six. We experience these emotions almost every day, if not every day.

There is, however, one that rises to the top multiple times a day, and that emotion is fear.

We live in a self-imposed condition of fear.

After all the other emotions have come and gone, fear remains.

We worry about the safety of our family, the possibility of losing our jobs, the loss of a loved one, and the fear of not being good enough. We're afraid of what people think of us , afraid of loneliness and abandonment; afraid we can't pay our bills; afraid of a health crisis for us or a loved one; afraid of someone hurting us, etc.

Beneath the façade of everything is fine, we're afraid; if things are going well, we believe that something bad is going to happen.

From the moment we wake up until our head hits the pillow, fear has run our life. If we allow it, fear will run our lives tomorrow and the day after that until we do something about it.

Here's a small prayer that I heard from Spirit, "Cleanse my thoughts, ease my fears, and erase my doubts."

Fear runs our lives until it ruins our lives.

Why this? Because our mindset has been conditioned to think negatively. This fear doesn't creep in; it's already there waiting for us to give it energy so it can take over. That's when the drumbeat begins, and as we fall deeper and deeper into a pit of despair, we look around and ask again, "Where did it all go wrong?" We all go through that, but the bigger question we should ask ourselves is, "Did it all really go wrong?" *Most of us are not afraid of failure but afraid of success.* If we believe that things are going to go wrong (and they will if we continue to manifest that negative energy), we say to ourselves, "I knew it. I knew I was going to fail." This normally happens when we try something once or twice and give up.

Great home run hitters have two things in common: 1) They strike out a lot, and 2) despite that, they keep swinging because they know that sooner or later, they will hit a home run.

(Understand that the above analogy seems to define the definition of insanity, which is doing the same thing repeatedly.) It's the law of averages that if you try to do something, and keep failing at it, success is just one swing away. Grab a bat and keep fear in the dugout where it belongs.

Here's a small prayer that I heard from Spirit. "Cleanse my thoughts, ease my fears, and erase my doubts."

In the Presence

These days, a popular phrase goes something like this, "Be in the present moment." (Actors identify with this phrase very well as they're rehearsing or preparing for a role.) Let us now take this phrase and change it a little. *Be in the presence moment.* This statement now carries significant and sacred energy, as it places us in the presence of a higher power. God's grace surrounds us wherever we are at this moment. Churches, temples, and sacred sanctuaries are special, but you don't have to go there to experience God's grace. It is all about energy. The chair we sit in has the presence of God. If we believe that God touches everything, then everything has "his" presence.

The book you are reading is the result of numerous handwritten drafts using a variety of pens, likely made by men and women of different backgrounds and cultures. Pens may seem insignificant to the casual observer, yet their presence facilitated the completion of this book. Men and women have built everything that surrounds us in our lives. Men and women who put energy into everything we use, buy, and perceive. The presence of their love and energy surrounds us. Can we not acknowledge that their presence makes our lives more enjoyable?

I'm not suggesting that we fall to our knees and start praying to a 2' by 4' piece of wood. I am, however, suggesting that there is a type of sacred energy in all that is around us. Our friends, acquaintances, family, loved ones, even those who don't like us, and vice versa, all symbolize the presence of something greater than ourselves.

Here's a lasting and sobering thought. Today will never repeat itself; the ups and downs, the highs, the lows, the situations we will find ourselves in, the people we meet, the people we saw but didn't give them a second look or even a glance, the places we went, the concrete, the grass, the trees, the buildings, the houses, the offices, the coffee shop, the waiter, the waitress, the phone calls, the children we played with, the family members we've engaged with, the traffic light that turned red, the rain that fell and ruined our golf game, or some other outdoor activity; all this and more will make for a beautiful, sacred, and presence-filled day.

We must slow down and appreciate the presence of something greater than ourselves. Let's embrace and enjoy tomorrow by taking some time to observe things and situations that were once overlooked. Everything is sacred, especially us.

The Old Self

When we go away for a period, we desire to return to a place that is familiar and comfortable for us. It's our home, our sanctuary, our dwelling place. Sometimes, when we return from an extended time away, we find things are not what they used to be. Energy has somehow changed. I'm not necessarily talking about physical places, although that plays into what we're discussing.

Think of our mind, body, and spirit as our home, our sanctuary, and our dwelling place. When our mind, body, and spirit go on a journey, either internal or external, and we long to return to the familiar, good old days, we find ourselves somewhat changed and start to panic about finding our way back. Could this be a sign that it's time to shed the skin of our old self and embrace the new skin? But sometimes we have this desire to put on the skin and mindset of our old self. In fact, people we once knew are no longer recognizable because their old selves are gone, but ours linger. Could it be, however, that upon further reflection, it's our old self that has departed and a new self has emerged? Perhaps the reason we don't recognize the ones that we thought we knew is because they appear different through our new lens?

The lens of our new self now sees that which was unrecognizable. No matter what we think of the person that we are, our new "you" has risen for a reason and now occupies our mind, body, and spirit. This means we are changing to see people and things in a new and different light. Some call this an awakening, while others see it as clarity to guide us on our path. At this point in our lives, we have shifted from our old selves to a more enlightened version of what we were meant to be.

Embrace this version, even if it may seem uncomfortable at first, because change is not easy to experience. The new self will now focus on our purpose and mission, enabling us to fulfill our soul's intended plan. Yes, there is a grand plan for our soul, given to us at birth for us to fulfill—a life full of excitement, enjoyment, and mystery. Let's do an exercise to better illustrate this: Take a sheet of paper, place it in front of you, and draw a line from the top to the bottom, dividing the paper in half. At the top, write your name, followed by the words OLD SELF on the left-hand side. Example: JERRY'S OLD SELF.

Then write your name and the words NEW SELF EXAMPLE: on the right-hand side. Take a pen and write down a few things that your old self did and did not accomplish and perhaps some things that you wanted to accomplish. Be true to yourself but don't be hard on yourself.

Again, no "yes, but…" answers here. Take a deep breath and write down things that have been accomplished and things that have yet to be accomplished. I'm sensing as I'm writing this that we all have accomplished things that weren't on the radar of our old selves.

I was a C student in high school, mainly because of my ADD. I was easily distracted, struggled to retain information, and couldn't focus. This meant that I didn't like to read, so books were a challenge for me. Yet here I am writing my third book, with more to come. I'm sure we all have stories that are like mine. Let's stand back and look at these lists with pride at what we have accomplished. As we can clearly see, there are no limits on what can be accomplished.

CHAPTER TWO

PATHWAYS

"If the path be beautiful, let us not ask where it leads."

—Anatole France

OVERVIEW

There are pathways and questions that the Universe would like us to contemplate. Can we duplicate a near-death experience? Are we people of wealth? Is the pain we feel self-inflicted? Do doors and windows lead to a non-physical world? Are there unseen forces that guide us? Do we have to land hard during difficult times? Is there a new age of metaphysical gifts that are upon us? Time to find out.

The God Helmet

The debate between science and spirituality has gone on for decades, if not centuries. Science exists for a couple of reasons: 1) To study the unknown, and 2) to accept or reject ideas depending upon the evidence presented. Science is at odds with spirituality more than spirituality is at odds with science. Attempts to put spirituality into a lab to dissect it, one particle at a time, have not resulted in desirable results.

Science isn't coldhearted or unfeeling. Science is just doing what it's supposed to be doing. Those of us who are of a spiritual nature are doing what we feel compelled to do. There have been numerous attempts by scientists to replicate a near-death experience (NDE) using a device called the "God Helmet." The God Helmet is a snowmobile helmet with electrodes attached to send electromagnetic waves to parts of the brain that are mostly affected by a lack of oxygen. These waves are designed to act as stimuli to those parts of the brain. They put subjects in a soundproof room, put the helmet on, and then put a blindfold on, so there is no sound other than an occasional brief comment from the control room telling them when the session starts and when the session ends. They are then sent the sequence of electromagnetic waves. Afterwards, the participants, some of whom had never had an NDE and those that had the NDEs, recall what they saw, felt, or heard.

There was success in duplicating emotions, sounds, images, and sensations. However, some things were missing. In these attempts at NDEs, several factors were often overlooked in the God's helmet sessions, such as the presence of the divine, the presence of our loved ones who have passed, the feeling of being connected to everything in the universe, etc. Note that some of these scientists do not believe that a soul or consciousness exists. Believe what you want to believe. They have their belief system, and we have ours.

Here are the factors that were not considered in the experiments.

1. The tunnel of light did not appear in many cases. This tunnel of light and colors that are unrecognizable are shared by many people who have had NDEs.
2. Not all actual NDEs are pleasant. Some reported that they had hellish experiences. This was not present in the sessions.
3. Many reported having a life review during their actual NDE. They watch the good and the not so good that have taken place in their lives. This also was not reported in the sessions.
4. Being in the presence of the divine or a divine being. This one resonates with many NDEs so clearly that they recall the feeling or the encounter.

This was not reported in many of the sessions. The aftereffects of an NDE seem to have been profound. Some of the people who have had these indicate their lives have changed or that they now see things differently. Others who were skeptical now fully believe in an afterlife.

Last, but not least, the experiments could not replace the experience. The sessions were successful in replicating feelings, sounds, lights, emotions, etc., but those do not constitute an experience. An experience happens in the present moment, which cannot be replicated nor explained. Again, the experiences that were listed above did not appear in the majority of what I've witnessed or read about. We can think back on experiences and recall them, but attempting to have that same exact experience almost never happens. Conditions, ambience, people, places, attitudes, etc., have all changed as we attempt to relive the experience. We may come close, but it is unlikely that we will be able to accurately recreate that experience in detail.

Science can create artificial intelligence but not consciousness.

This is mainly because many scientists' belief system prohibits them from doing so. Will science pull off a detailed and accurate NDE? Maybe, but given the attitudes of those who cannot keep an open mind regarding NDEs or the soul/consciousness, it's highly doubtful. You must have an open mind and a zero agenda mentality when conducting the God Helmet sessions, just like you would if you ran the sessions with the belief that NDEs did exist and you secretly wanted the experiment to fail.

The people who have had NDEs know what they experienced. and no laboratory experiment, as detailed as the God Helmet sessions were, will alter or change what they saw, heard, and felt during their visit to the other side. The Divine has an energy of its own, but we do not have to have a near-death experience to feel it or sense it. Every day we are surrounded by divine energy that never leaves us; no helmet is needed.

Abundance Never Falters

"Abundance" has many definitions. One of the more widely accepted ones is "having more than we need." Some people define abundance as money, property, stocks, bonds, a big house, cars, and so on.

There are other definitions, especially for people who have never had much, not even basic necessities. To those folks, having enough food on the table means an abundance of blessings. Having clothes on our backs and a roof over our heads signifies an early Christmas for some.

There's a clip online from several years ago where a gentleman decides to treat some homeless men to a Super Bowl party. He gives them New England jerseys, hats, and the whole nine yards. When it came time for the group to go through the buffet line, they all loaded up their plates with food and took them back to their table. A curious thing then happened. The homeless bowed their heads and gave thanks while the entire party (this was at a big hotel bar) drank and ate and did all the things that you normally do at a Super Bowl party. Yet the homeless were the ones to pause and give thanks. For them, this was an abundant feast, and they remembered how to give thanks for their blessings, even though in the next 3–4 hours they would be back on the street. They recognized abundance in its simplest form. The question is, do we?

Abundance has an energy of its own, waiting for someone to recognize it and appreciate it. There is an abundance of love which never ever falters or falls short of accomplishing its goal.

We have much to offer to those who have little.

Those who are homeless are not bums, alcoholics, or anything of the sort. First, nobody is a bum; the Creator doesn't "make" bums. Second, yes, some are alcoholics and the like, but others are not and just fall into a pit of despair. When abundance shows up to all of us, some of us, including myself, failed to recognize it, so we overlook it. Could it be time for us to stop being a problem and start becoming a solution?

So, where is God in all of this? How come God allows this misery in the world, such as homelessness, despair, and the like? God does not allow this. We do. We are abundant in resources. Where are we in this scenario? Why can't we help? Even if we don't have much, I'm confident most of the people reading this have a phone. A phone call to someone that we haven't talked to in a while just to share our abundance of love, mercy, and positive energy is all someone needs. We are being called to help others who could use some abundance on their path, just like others helped us on ours. Or did we forget that abundance of generosity? We all know someone who could use a small gesture of abundance. This is our legacy.

Trauma Triggers

We all have trauma/pain points installed all over our mind, body, and spirit. What is the trigger and how did it get there? Triggers are a gentle and sometimes not so gentle reminder of something negative in our past. This can happen in any situation or people that we encounter as it brings that pain to the surface. It causes us to relive, even for a moment, pain that either we forgot about or would just soon go away. When this happens, we say to ourselves "I cannot believe this is happening! Why is this happening to me, just as everything is going ok?" How did we arrive at this point in our lives, where triggers of trauma bring back haunted memories of people, places, and things that went wrong? We made a solemn vow to ourselves that we would put these situations behind us.

We must acknowledge the traumas in our lives that are self-imposed.

We need to take ownership of that and seek some resolution around this trauma, which we inadvertently apply to our lives. So, what are the purposes of these triggers? Could it be to remind us not to go down the same path as before? Could it also be that in these triggers we had a hand in it, and perhaps that's why we would soon forget them? Let's be honest, we know very well there are situations and people in our lives that we initiated the action or discussion, and it ended very badly on the part of others. The fact remains, however, that we started it. Taking ownership of this trauma is when we start to grow as a person. It's not easy, but growth never is.

We are not talking about the pain of losing a loved one. That pain needs to stay for as long as you want it to. Nobody has the right to tell anyone, "You need to let go of that" or "You've mourned enough; time to get over it." No one walks the same path, so grieving and mourning is personal to everyone, which makes the process challenging. In trauma, there are no stages. The purpose of revisiting these pain points or triggers is to teach us a lesson.

The renowned Franciscan mystic, Fr. Richard Rohr, says it best: "I like to ask pain, what are you trying to teach me?" This is a man who has had cancer many times, had a major heart attack, and is in his seventies. After acknowledging our part in some of this pain, let us claim it, and make a promise to correct our actions.

To those who have caused us pain, we do not claim ownership of their issues or their pain.

That is their path, not ours. Ironically, these pain points come to the surface when we least expect it. We perceive this as extremely annoying and frustrating, yet the Universe brings pain into our lives at crucial moments to help us reconcile it and discover the lesson we still need to learn. Maybe the Universe sees where we're heading and wants to remind us of a previous path that we took that didn't end well. Higher forces, or a higher power, are helping us along our path. Take solace in knowing that forgiving others and ourselves is grace. By talking to our pain, maybe we will understand it a little better.

I was fortunate enough to co-facilitate a Richard Rohr men's retreat several years ago in Winter Park, Florida. One of the exercises we did was to put a six-foot crucifix of Jesus on the floor, take as many post-it notes as we wanted, and, reflecting upon our own trauma and pain, we then put the notes on the body of Jesus to correspond to the places where our trauma and pain were. This was to illustrate the healing power of Jesus, with the hope that he would carry our cross of pains and help us on our path of trauma. It was also understood that this included our self-inflicted trauma and pain.

I understand not everyone who reads this book is Christian or has a relationship with Jesus that many do. This serves as a simple example of acknowledging the pain and trauma in we experience in our lives, particularly the self-imposed pain points and trauma triggers.

Soft Landings

I overheard a conversation once, where someone mentioned heading for a soft landing. I remembered this conversation, and with a slight push from the Universe, this became the title of this book and, at the same time, became the direction of the writings as well.

What does it mean to have a soft landing? Could it mean that when we fall, we are hoping to find a cushion, symbolically and literally? The cushion could be a family member, friend, co-worker, or even a stranger just wanting to help upon seeing us fall and not wanting to see us land hard or hit rock bottom. Sometimes our falls are fast; other times, not so much. But this much is true: Some of the falls we see coming and some we don't, but no matter the fall, we all need a soft landing.

A soft landing puts us on our path to find our center of balance.

Soft landings teach us to help others find their balance as well. We think we're prepared for all possibilities, but we don't know what is waiting for us around the corner. We can hope and pray that someone will be there to help us by cushioning the fall. Once we land, hopefully we'll have help getting up and moving forward.

The flip side of that coin is the question: When have we been there for people who have fallen? More importantly, have we cushioned the fall for our friends and family without passing judgment? When we fall, it's like a dark chapter in our lives. Helping those who have fallen and providing a soft landing for them is like a ray of sunshine in their lives. Let's continue that work and take a minute to reflect upon those who helped us on our path. What did they do to lend a hand? Was it a word of encouragement? A phone call perhaps? A text message? A cup of coffee away from home or work? Helping with the family somehow? Picking up or dropping off the kids? Perhaps helping with a few (a few) dollars to help buy groceries? There are several areas in which we have been helped, so why not return the favor?

There was a person (who shall remain nameless) who asked me for a favor, which I was glad to do, as it only took about 20 minutes. Four months later, I asked this person for a favor in about the same time frame, only to hear that this person was too busy to help. It's great to help people out, and even better not to expect anything in return. I didn't expect anything in return, but sometimes we do need a little help. I didn't frame it as "you owe me" because I didn't think for a moment that I was owed anything. I just needed a little help in one area. This person responded with a short sentence, "I'm too busy."

I have never heard anything from this person since, but that's okay. I wish this person well and have received a little help from someone else. If we're all in this together, let's hold up our end of the bargain. When someone helps us, let's be open to the opportunity to help them when they need it. Not expecting anything in return and locating soft landing spots for others is a true act of grace, and it's up to us to extend that grace.

The New Breed

Before things of metaphysical nature were written about or even discussed, there was a mystery surrounding this material that resulted in finger-pointing and claims of devil-worshipping. No one discussed topics like tarot, mediumship, psychic abilities, clairvoyance, etc., until books on these subjects began to appear not only in small independent metaphysical stores but also in larger ones. These books could be found in major bookstore chains in the "occult" section, alongside books about witches, warlocks, and Ouija boards. (For the record, I don't use Ouija boards.) Then the metaphysical books were elevated to the "New Age" section, making them more mainstream.

Then, they became as mainstream as they could be, finding their place in the "Self-Transformation" section, where they should have been all along. This Self-Transformation section now includes astrology, numerology, and spiritual books as well. This New Age of Self-Transformation also means a new age of old souls. This transformation of spiritual awakening is evident everywhere, especially in old souls whose gifts may have been lying dormant. These old souls mean they have discovered their metaphysical gifts and truly embraced them.

Old souls keep an open mind on everything and everyone and sometimes have knowledge and wisdom beyond their years.

They realize this by embracing these self-transformational gifts; they have a meaning and purpose to use these gifts to help people in need. This is their mission in life.

We have all met these people. They normally occupy a place at the back of the room, almost going unnoticed, remaining calm in the middle of chaos. Their energy exudes calmness, peace, sincerity, and steadiness.

They are the healers and empaths of the world who go about their day-to-day business unnoticed because their mission and purpose in life is to heal the world, one soul at a time. It is as if their energy represents a small, single drop of sacred glue, holding people and situations together. They are the new breeds of old souls who have become more prominent since the year 2000, awakening like a universal sleeper cell to aid the world, one precious soul at a time. Is there a situation that needs your healing touch? What would it take to help in this situation?

Take a moment and breathe in your God-given gifts, visualizing how you can help. Now breathe out and go. We are being called to keep an open mind on things that are not easily understood. The question is: Could you be one of those who bring calm and common sense to (tense) situations, thereby bringing hatred and negativity to its knees so positivity can be the lesson of the day? Our gifts are needed. What are we going to do? Time to get to work, but let's not listen to reply (thank you, Stephen Covey) when we're engaged with an old soul. We must learn to listen in order to understand (again, thanks Stephen Covey).

Everyday Portals

There are various words to describe what a portal is: passage, gateway, entrance, entry, and so on. The words that stand out to me, however, are doors and windows. These are openings to other environments. Why would we look at these everyday occurrences as portals? When we're leaving our dwelling place and going outside or coming back from the outside to the inside, we leave energy behind and come into an environment of new energy. Windows serve a similar purpose, as we regularly open the windows and close them without thinking about the energy we are releasing and the energy that is entering. Doors and windows as everyday portals? Why not? Celtic folklore views oak trees as a site of transition from life to death.

Look at it this way: energy is everything; it is all around us and in us. Inside our bodies is an energy field; inside our homes are energy fields. Outside our homes are countless energy fields. Some are better than others. If we accept the premise that portals lead us to other dimensions, and that dimensions are energy fields, some good and some not so good, then looking at doors and windows as portals to other energy fields starts to make sense. What is a dimension? It is mainly a combination of time and space, but many other things as well. Windows and doors allow us to explore those areas of time and space. Like windows and doors, dimensions allow us, if we're open to them, to move from one clean space to another.

Portals, levels, realms, dimensions, layers of energy—whatever we want to call them—allow us to move freely and come and go as we please. What we need is a password of some sort to enter these portals. Our password is "open mind." When we open a door or window, we need to have an open mind. When we walk outside and close the door behind us, we do enter a space of hope… of starting anew and fresh, depending upon when we leave. It's as if we're leaving a sanctuary and entering a world that hopefully will be good, even though there's negative energy all around us. Our dwelling place should be a sanctuary, but to some it's exactly the opposite.

To some, their home is anything but a sanctuary. Abuse, in many shapes and forms, is the dominant energy in the home. To them, home is merely a building with negative, angry, cruel energy, and nothing more. Leaving the building and going outside may be their sanctuary. Wherever home is, dreams are there to be formed, and plans can be made to realize them. Again, to others, the building they inhabit doesn't create enough space for dreams to be realized, much less formed. To those who don't have the opportunity to have dreams, the building they live in is more like a prison.

Their portals are waiting for them elsewhere, and the door they walk through will embrace them with positive energy.

Windows give us an opportunity to breathe in fresh air and breathe out whatever drama, tension, or pain that we might be holding inside us or inside the house. Windows allow us to hear sounds such as nature, birds, trees, and even cars honking and traffic. To hear people going about their daily routines does allow us to dream and wonder what people are doing with their lives. Nothing wrong with dreaming as long as our two feet are on the ground with our own dreams, ideas, plans, and goals.

Opening a window and/or door also can bring in negative energy from the outside world. How do we prevent these energies from coming in or, worse, attach themselves to us? Anyone who protects their family will also protect their home.

Negative energies are like barnacles, and they can attach to us. Saying a prayer of protection before we go outside or even open a window gives us confidence that negative energies will not enter and will stay away. It sounds complicated, but it's nothing but a simple prayer such as "Spirit, please protect me from negative energies today."

Putting intentions behind prayer is the path to the divine.

Look at it this way… We walk out the door feeling good, maybe even great, and by lunchtime we start to feel down, depressed, and out of sorts. By the time we come home, our energy is drained. What happened to us throughout the day that caused us to behave and act the way we did? Negative energy somehow infiltrated our lives, possibly regurgitating rumors, negative stories, thoughts, actions, etc. This is especially true for empaths, who are very sensitive to all kinds of energy, especially within people.

Every door, every window is an opening or closing to another portal of energy, again, either positive or negative. Energies are everywhere and if we recognize that, every opening we walk through presents new energy, new opportunities, and new challenges. It's all about the energy around us and in us.

As Nikola Tesla puts it, "If you want to find the secrets of the Universe, think in terms of energy, frequency, and vibration." Doors, like portals, are meant to be opened and closed. That's why they were built in the first place. We were meant to go through them and close them behind us. That's why we were made—to navigate, explore, and raise our awareness about the world around us and perhaps discover the sacred energy that is out there and in here.

Who Guides Us?

There are times we feel guided by someone or something that seems to be of a higher power or nature. It is hard to describe, but somewhere deep inside us we have a feeling, a voice, a déjà vu moment which comes to us when we least expect it and when we need it the most. It could be an angel, guardian angel, a loved one who has passed on, etc.

The feeling or sensation that seems to be the loudest comes from our intuition, and that part of our spirit, soul, or consciousness is a megaphone for what we call our "spirit guide." We have many spirit guides as they were "assigned" (or volunteered) when we were born. We all have a multitude of guides: healing guides, messenger guides, and many other types of guides.

Everyone has guides that come and go into our lives at various times.

Again, many of them appear at crucial moments. Even if we're an atheist, agnostic, or unlabeled non-believer, we all know that feeling that we get.

There are also enlightened beings and figures such as Jesus, Mary, Blessed Mother, God, Mary Magdalen, Buddha, Mohammed, and so on. In the spirit realm where these beings of love and light dwell, there are no divisions of religion, so even if we are non-believers these spirit guides are with us. They try to put us on the path of non-duality, the path that enlightens and doesn't divide our mind into black and white.

Those are all vibrations from our spirit guides. They guide us toward the correct path; even if we keep pushing back and go on other paths, they are always with us.

How often do we go about contacting these guides? Spirit guides, like archangels but not as highly ascended, are beings who once walked the earth, just like you and me, with some minor exceptions. In most cases, but not all, we don't know them in our current life, as some are from countries that we've never visited and can even be hundreds of years old.

It is difficult to imagine talking, carrying on a conversation, or having a thought about these entities and sacred souls who help guide us on our path. It's okay to turn to our loved ones who have passed and reflect on the influence they had and continue to have on our lives. But how do we contact them? Dim the lights, light a candle, and just say hello to your spirit guides. Our guides love it when we are patient; so let us show patience. In the end, grace is plentiful.

Our loved ones also reach out and guide us, even if we're not aware of them. I'm sure all of us have turned to those we've lost and asked for help, guidance, answers, or just to say hello. If we are of a particular religion, I'm confident that we can turn to Jesus, Mary Magdalene, Mary, the Blessed Mother, Buddha, Mohammed, Kwan Yin, Sanat Kamara, White Tara, Serapis Bey, or any ascended master for assistance, grace, mercy, comfort, and clarity to help us on our path.

Spirit guides are no different although they have not evolved of a higher vibration than Jesus and the others that I mentioned, such as archangels and angels, who are of a higher vibration, but the energy, love, and desire to assist are still there. Connecting to our spirit guides requires patience and commitment, as it is a habit that takes time to develop.

Just sit for a few minutes in the beginning, have patience, and verbalize your intentions to connect with your spirit guides. You may not connect right away, but after a dozen or so years of doing readings, I still don't see my guides, even though I know they're there. Other mediums see them, but I don't because we all connect in different ways. Our spirit guides are waiting to connect and all we must do is find a place of solitude and listen with an open heart. It will take time and patience, but trust me they are there, and, in some way, they will make their presence known.

CHAPTER THREE

LANDSCAPES

"I like this place and could willingly waste my time in it."

—William Shakespeare

OVERVIEW

In this chapter, we explore and discuss subjects such as injustice, conformity, non-conformity, confrontations, expectations, good places, the circus of a different color, and conflict in different and intriguing ways. An open mind is necessary to understand what Spirit is trying to say to us. Bend your thoughts, and the soul will follow.

Eye of Injustice

Every day, we all have a front-row seat to watch an alarming scenario played out for us to see. This scenario is called injustice. Injustice flaunts its negative energy like a buzzard spreading its wings and looking for victims. It flies low as to hide amongst us, peering around, almost daring us to do something about it. Yes, we sometimes see injustice on a large scale, like a company not taking care of its workers or a country imprisoning its citizens.

As far as injustice is concerned, there are no innocent bystanders. All of us, at one time or another, are bystanders. Whether we are innocent or not is up to us. We all get caught up in situations where we witness something happening that isn't quite right, or our gut (intuition) tells us that something is wrong. We're not talking about intervening when our intuition tells us to step back. Intuition is never wrong; it will not steer us in the wrong direction. What we fail to do is listen to our intention regarding acting or not acting on behalf of someone or a situation. When we see something that isn't right, we won't deceive ourselves. More times than not, when something appears unusual, it truly is.

Our eyes are the windows to the soul, as someone once said, and our soul alerts us when things are not what they appear to be. Our eyes do not deceive us; it's our thoughts that deceive us.

If we observe something that seems to be an injustice and a pit in our stomach or chest appears, it is time to take cautious action. Injustice rears its ugly head at street level, one person at a time. Now, we're not talking about running into a hail of bullets or a gang fight. When we see injustice, such as those who are homeless, hungry, jobless, etc., we are called by a higher power to apply justice, peace, and understanding to the situation or person. Racism and discrimination are areas that are so visible we cannot hide from them, but a majority of this happens in small, dark areas.

Those areas are as prevalent today as they were centuries ago. We cannot pretend they don't exist or conclude that things will get better and go away. We all know that's not going to happen. If we are to get involved at any level, we should say a quick prayer of protection to Archangel Michael, God Infinite Intelligence, or any other spirit from the highest realms for protection as we go forth and try to make the world a better place.

Gathering the Dust

See if this resonates. There's a heated argument between two friends, and while we're outside watching and listening, we feel the need to intervene, as we hate to see friends go at it. Let's look at the same scenario, but this time with family members yelling at each other on their latest "I can't stand you" tour, which seems to never end. This hurts even more because the bloodline is there, but the bond is broken.

Just as we feel the need to step forward and quietly intervene with a word or two, the two participants, or better yet, combatants, disengage and leave the arena they were in, retreating to their corners or the other side of the house.

The conflict is over, and the confrontation has taken its toll. We stood by and watched people that we love and care for go toe-to-toe to the brink of absolute destruction. This relationship has just gone down in flames. If we consider ourselves to be healers, then an overwhelming sense of failure may consume us because, in our minds, we did not do anything to stop this. I must say that at this point, I'm speaking of verbal disagreements, not physical ones. Physical ones are an entirely different matter. These situations call for all-hands-on-deck approach to prevent an escalation that could turn deadly.

Back to the verbal situation. They've left, so now what? Healing in this case comes in three phases: 1) Healing before the confrontation gets heated; 2) Healing during the confrontation; 3) Healing after the confrontation. Which of the scenarios I presented at the beginning of this chapter is the most important for healing? The answer is after the confrontation. Situations like these are dangerous because they involve anger.

Breathing life to anger gives birth to bitterness.

Bitterness sometimes lasts forever, whereas anger can be fleeting if we offer healing in our own way. Our role as trusted friends or family members is not to fix the situation. Both need love, prayers, and healing separately, not together. We've all seen situations where both parties are brought together to "clear the air" and go through a conflict resolution. It looks good in movies and TV shows, but we know that those are tricky waters to navigate. We're not called to intervene, even if we're therapists or counselors. We're called to gather the dust of the feelings, emotions, and hurtful language that was used and send it to the Universe with a quick prayer or meditation. We need to give these folks space to breathe. They do not need us to blow up their phone with our wisdom and knowledge.

We are not experts on other people's lives.

They have ownership of their own lives; we don't. Maybe one day they will do some work with perhaps reflections or inner healing. There is also the reality that we all fear: that reconciliation is not possible or probable. This could last for years or even a lifetime. Again, what do we do? Healing energy has a life of its own, and we don't know how, when, or if it works in cases such as this. Our mistake is thinking there's no healing if we don't see the results we expect.

Healing has many layers and comes in many forms that we never witness.

Our task is to be available when they want to talk and just listen. That's part of gathering the dust, sending love and light to each one, and continuing to do so even if it's not the outcome we desire. Moving forward with healing is what we're called to do.

Off Script

Throughout our lives, whether we believe it or not, we are given scripts for us to live by. Our parents, loved ones, spouse, children, friends, co-workers, and acquaintances give us these scripts, and depending upon how thick and heavy these scripts are, we think, talk, and act accordingly.

The minute we attempt to go on our own and think, talk, and act the way we want to or have always wanted to, we are told "no, no, no." If we continue to go "rogue" and not follow the rules and the marching orders, we are going to hear lectures, and we are all guilty of that. How do others know that we are not doing our best? How do they know we are not trying as hard as we can? But, somehow, based on the small and trivial things we've accomplished in the past, they seem to have insight and knowledge of our inner being. We're again reminded that we can do better. Don't they know we just wish they would either be quiet or go away? It is almost tempting to tell the world, "I'm leaving home to go into the real world to experience failure and fulfill the prophecy." (Just kidding.)

I would bet my last dollar that many artists, poets, musicians, singers, sculptors, hairdressers, writers, and so on were at one point told to abandon their dreams and get a job. Join the family business, and we do, but we daydream about becoming rappers as we write about the anger, hurt, and disappointment that we have felt inside us and others.

Going off script means we have a voice to change the world.

There are risks to doing this, so we all need to weigh these risks on a scale next to the word "timing." When is the time right?

By meditating and listening to our intuition and feeling that little urge or push, we will all know when it is time to go off the various scripts that we have been handed in throughout our lives. Some of us will go slowly, while others will take the plunge and jump off the paper trail that has been following us all these years. Let's write down three or more things that we want to accomplish in life—things that we want to do, not what everyone tells us to do, but our dreams, goals, and aspirations that are deep within us.

The only way to bring these dreams to fruition is to believe in them, thereby putting positive energy into them. Let's not let go of these dreams if we're serious about achieving them. Going off script takes courage, commitment, and conviction. Weigh the risk but have the courage to throw away the scripts.

Here Comes the Circus

The finger pointers and naysayers that we have all experienced in our lifetimes seem to get larger and louder as we age. It never stops, never slows down, and makes space for judgment to come roaring in. Where did this start? How did it happen? How do we recognize it when it happens? This is one of several common themes throughout this book. That theme is to be a non-conformist on most things and not buy into the mob mentality.

When we experience a moment of inspiration and clarity that may not exist with others, we buckle up. They are coming for us. Who or what are they? It is the circus, and they are not too happy with us, especially when we enjoy success without their permission and/or their blessing.

They hear about it through the coconut telegraph from family members and friends. We forgot to genuflect at their altar of approval. Shame on us. We should know better. So, they come, pitching their tents outside our house to teach us to never draw outside the lines, even if it means we have found success. Is this jealousy? Perhaps, but there seems to be something underneath this layer. These are the people closest to us, which makes these scenarios surreal. They arrive in cars, trucks, vehicles, bicycles, unicycles (it's a circus after all), skateboards, planes, helicopters, you name it, they come. Let us not forget that we all do the same at various stages of our lives. Is it a competition? That could be because the world is competitive in every way, but it seems more than that.

Let us flip to the other side of the coin for a minute and talk about what we do to others. Human behavior is one of the strangest and hardest to define or explain. Let's be honest, as little kids and even as we reached adulthood, we all wanted to run away, maybe to even join the circus. That could be at the heart of this. We ran away to join or even start our own circus and not theirs. Why do we do the things we do? Why do we find or seek pleasure in slicing and dicing through people's lives when they take a turn that we cannot understand or don't approve of?

Why do we have to understand people having success in ways that we didn't anticipate? When is it our turn? We've been good and deserve it, haven't we? Why does our universe seem to be ripped in shreds when things don't align with our blueprint for what we call our perfect world? After all, we know everything about everybody, as we have had their lives all planned out for years. This usually comes just as we are convinced that we have everything figured out. Right now is when we will receive an invitation in the mail. Someone from the circus is throwing a pity party in our honor.

We must refuse invitations from anyone's pity parties, including our own.

Once we feel we have accomplished our mission to reset their lives back into the comfortable chair that we are used to seeing them in, the circus starts to pack up their tents and head to the next town to find that person who just isn't cooperating with them because they came and conquered. In our case, they leave behind a ton of trash resembling dreams, ideas, and aspirations that we thought were good and hopeful as we continue our path(s) in life. Earlier I mentioned that it could be jealousy, but underneath lies another agenda. In most cases, we did it alone and didn't invite them to participate.

"Why didn't you tell me what you were going to do? I would have understood." Really? I think we know better. When an original thought or plan pops into our heads, we want to see it to its end.

Bottom line: This usually happens when we are in the process of evolving into an idea of greater and deeper understanding, and the performers from the circus aren't at that place of inner awakening. One day, we hope they will be. All of this is a shakeup in our energy and the people around us. Well-intentioned as they are, they don't understand or don't want to understand us or the sacred space we now occupy. We have our path; they have theirs. It's that simple.

Ancient Ways

In the past decades and centuries, there were villages that were self-sustaining communities and had to follow certain rules to sustain, grow, and nurture life within them. These communities were home to wise, knowledgeable elders who served as a foundation for young men, women, and children to develop into active adults who could contribute to society and become active citizens of the world.

When there was a problem or situation in the community, these elders gave wise and insightful advice. They were the shamans, the mystics, the alchemists, the patriarchs, matriarchs, and mentors of the community. They were tasked with the responsibility of carrying forward the ancient ways so that everyone who grew up and left the villages would do the same.

These ancient ways included honoring the mother and father with an additional emphasis on grandparents. Respect for elders and an unwavering unconditional desire to pitch in and assist the community were also part of the ancient ways. They were mentors, most of them old souls, which explains where a good deal of wisdom came from. Elders were not old people who just leaned against an old shack while falling asleep, only to occasionally wake up to tell a young person to quit throwing rocks at the house. Sadly, in the Western part of the world we have forgotten that and refer to elders as old fools who just don't understand how the modern world works. There are fewer and fewer elders in today's world because they feel that they are no longer wanted. The elders didn't tell the people in these communities what to do. They were very much like Jesus (not trying to be sacrilegious) in that they told stories or parables to illustrate why things were done a certain way and the nature of reality. In addition, they gave advice as to ways to work in the world and what they could do to impact change.

The elders were and still are the legacy holders of the planet.

Today, villages are more global and connected. The knowledge that our elders imparted to us as lessons to learn and then pass on to the next generation gave us hope back in the day. So, where are today's elders? Why can't it be us? We don't necessarily have to be old these days to be one. We only need wisdom, knowledge, and grace, which a lot of us have. We need the ability to sit down and listen without judgment. Our voices need to be heard, not by shouting through a megaphone, but in a whisper. Elders speak in hushed tones, one on one, or in a small circle. Elders speak quietly, much like the ancient ways. We won't find them in churches, temples, or synagogues. Their life is their ministry, and they do this at ground level because that's where the people are. God bless these men and women of unwavering but quiet faith. Let's seek out those who have had a major positive influence in our lives and sit with them one more time to inhale that knowledge and wisdom so we can pass it on by exhaling that breath to someone else.

Good Places

When we run into someone who we care about, one of the first questions we normally ask is how they are doing. The responses we receive vary in length and degree of passion. Of course, the most common response we receive is that they are fine. The response that maybe most of us want to hear is that they are in a good place.

That's about as good as it gets in life—that we find ourselves in a good place. Through trauma, disappointments, disasters, unfulfilled dreams, hard work, etc., we somehow found a path to a good place, a sanctuary of sorts that creates a sacred space for us to unwind and re-energize.

What factors contribute to finding a good place? Those previously mentioned and more. That place can be physical, spiritual, or mental; you get the picture. A good place has energy of its own, and speaking of ownership, we own it and nobody else. It's ours to relish, ask questions to ourselves and perhaps a higher power, or just sit and meditate with no expectations other than to quiet ourselves. It might take some time for us to find our place, our sanctuary, but find it we must because we need that sacred energy.

This raises the question: "What do we do once we find good places?" Perhaps it's time to help others find their places. When people come to us with their problems, it's a good time to listen without interrupting, and then offer a suggestion, "Here's what I do when I come face to face with trauma." Then we let the suggestion lie there and hopefully at some point it will rise to the surface. What we were doing at that time was sharing a gift. It could help someone, but it surely cannot hurt. *A gentle suggestion goes much further than a marching order.*

If we think back and open the memory bank, maybe someone made the same suggestion to us. Knowledge is gentle. Here's a thought: we've been talking about good places, but what about the places (non-dangerous) that we would prefer not to go to? These places may need our energy to transform their environment. There is wisdom in the desert that needs our energy. Let's go find it.

Winds of Expectations

Throughout our lives, there are numerous sets of expectations placed upon us. Our family and loved ones instill certain expectations in us. As we grow older, we encounter expectations placed upon us from a diverge set of friends, co-workers at our jobs, and people we fall in love with. Finally, as we get older, we decide to put in place our own set of expectations. In the work of mediumship and clairvoyance, loved ones sometimes come through to reassure the person that they have surpassed all expectations that were put upon them. We want loved ones, friends, and communities to be proud of us as we try to live up to their expectations.

We can feel drained trying to live up to everyone's expectations.

If we had to list those expectations in order of importance, take an educated guess: whose expectations finish last? Ours! Expectations are like the wind; they blow in and out. We just need to know which ones to catch and which ones to release. The ones we hold onto are the ones that are meaningful to us and us alone. Poets, artists, musicians, athletes, and many others at one point were told to pursue other career paths. Sometimes we succeed; sometimes we fall short. The thing that happens is that we try new things that free our soul, and it doesn't matter how people judge what we do. What matters is that we learn things about life and, more importantly, ourselves. What happens if our financial goals aren't met? Don't get me wrong, nobody wants to lose money, but sometimes the path we choose that leads to a dead end isn't a failure.

The winds of the Universe gently blow us on a side street that we don't pick up in time, and so we forge ahead. We come to that dead end or wall and start to curse ourselves for being so stupid to think of a ridiculous idea. Meanwhile, the Universe is trying to tell us, "Go back and look at the journey, for your true destination or calling is in there. We just had to get you on the path first." Then we hear others tell us, "Keep your expectations realistic."

When it comes to goal setting, the word realistic is a code word for average. If our expectations are average, then so will the results be. Even in an industry such as sales, we are given stretch goals because a good manager or leader knows there is more in us to achieve them for the company and our financial success. This is because goals and expectations are two different species within the same jungle. They co-exist somewhat peacefully until expectations decide to go it alone for two sets of goals to be met…the company's and ours.

We need to believe in ourselves and our dreams, because the dream world, either asleep or awake, is the incubator for our expectations. To achieve it, we need to expect the best for ourselves. Let's start each day with one expectation that we set for ourselves and then ask ourselves, "What if I went beyond what is expected of me? What should I expect of myself?"

Our destiny has a soul, so let's talk to it: "Show me a path and teach me how to get there."

CHAPTER FOUR

Awakening

"The greater the doubt, the greater the awakening."

—Albert Einstein

OVERVIEW

Awakening and spiritual wisdom are one and the same. This chapter explores subjects such as invitations, helping our loved ones who have passed, the routines in our lives, being told what to do, the soul, and the past. This chapter was and still is a true awakening for me, and I hope it is for you and yours. Thank you, Spirit.

A Standing Invitation

We are gifted people; it's part of our universal DNA. It's our legacy, our responsibility, our heritage, and our mission to discover these gifts and use them. As descendants of gifted people, it is our duty to properly use these gifts (gifts of healing, patience, understanding, wisdom, knowledge, compassion, and listening, among others).

These gifts become "activated" when we use them to help others on their path. If we don't start to use them, they lie dormant for years, struggling to get to the surface. They are meant to be shared so that others might use them to "activate" their own gifts to help people. There is no need to ask for these gifts from the Creator. All of us have a standing invitation to use them, but the desire must be there. We must *want* to use them.

What about other people's gifts? There is no need to look at them and wonder why we don't have the same gifts as they do. They have their gifts; we have ours. No need to compare or become jealous.

Jealousy is not a gift, so there is no need to embrace it.

It will hinder those gifts that we have. Gifts from "above" are meant to be used repeatedly, not saved for special occasions. How do we know what our gifts are? Think back to when we've helped someone or somebody. What gifts did we use to bring much-needed light to that situation? Have we done this repeatedly throughout our lives to help people? Are there other gifts that we can use to help others? When have we seen people we know showing love, compassion, caring, or taking action to help others? Did we sit back, observe, and ask ourselves, "Why can't I do that?" Perhaps we wished we had gifts that we could use to help others. We have so many gifts to help others *and* ourselves.

In big and little ways, we've helped so many people find their way to a better path in life. For example, a friend or family member calls us because they've had a difficult day and there's no one to talk to, so you listen. We may think it's not a big deal, but the person on the other end probably sees it differently. How many times has somebody listened to us and we thought "I'm so glad they were there for us."

Being a friend is a gift often overlooked.

Here are some other gifts that are taken for granted. The gift of a smile. The gift of a kind word. The gift of a compliment. The gift of our presence. The gift of advice. The gift of encouragement. The gift of a meal. The gift of inviting a friend to lunch. The gift of a whisper. The gift of compassion. The gift of answering the phone when no one else would. The gift of not quitting on people. The gift of lending a hand. If we don't recognize the times we've stopped to assist others, then we are truly gifted individuals, as we perform these actions without thinking. We use these gifts all the time without realizing it. Let's now add the grace of sacred intentions into our efforts to help those who in need. After we lend a helping hand, let's ask the Universe or pray that others do the same. After all, we could be in a long chain of help. Let's not break the chain. Who knows, we might be the first to start a brand-new chain for others to follow. Whether we continue a chain or start a new one, let's use our energy for others to follow.

Rest In Peace

When we say goodbye to a loved one and tell them to "rest in peace," it is our one desire that they will find peace and happiness in the afterlife, if we believe that such a thing exists. Our part in their passing and crossing over to a higher realm or dimension, however, is not done. We must live our lives the best we can for our loved ones to truly rest in peace. It's all about vibrations. We will send more higher vibrations to the afterlife the more good deeds we perform, such as thinking positively, being non-judgmental, and speaking well of others. "Kindness surgeries" are how we can operate daily to make our loved ones proud of us in the afterlife and the work that we do.

It's the same as when we meet people and can tell whether we get a good or bad feeling about them. How many times have we said or thought to ourselves, "I'm getting a bad vibe about him or her?"

Vibrations or vibes are not only how we recognize the good and the not-so-good in people but also in ourselves. Positive vibrations are drawn to our soul like bees to honey.

Acts of kindness, showing patience, smiling to people that we don't know, helping those who do not have much—you get the idea. Our loved ones who have crossed over are near us more than we realize. They express great satisfaction in how we live our lives and some slight disappointment in what we have done and continue to do. Don't get me wrong; their ascension into a higher realm or dimension (whom some call Heaven) does not depend on what we do. Their ascension depends on what kind of life they led when they were here on Earth. However, knowing that we are making them proud in what we do and how we treat others raises our own vibrations so that the legacy of high vibrations continues in our bloodline of energy.

Energy is a two-way street in that people who have passed are still raising their vibrations to obtain more knowledge, wisdom, light, whatever you want to call it, for them to reach higher dimensions. When a loved one is in the afterlife, they continue to strive to ascend for their own enlightenment and ours. The higher they go, the more they can help us here on Earth. Help us by being near us in our times of sorrow, appearing in our dreams to comfort us, sending us signs to show that they are near; the list is endless. This is why energy is a two-way stream.

Resting in peace is the start of their afterlife, and that energy is passed down. Consider this: We walk into a house that was occupied by a loved one who passed and say, "I can still feel Grandmother's energy." That pretty much sums it up.

A Routine Driven Life

We get up, get dressed, go to work or wherever, fight traffic or turn on our computers in our home office, and then go back to our family life or, if we live alone, our regular daily routine. We are, for the most part, gifted but trapped people in society. Some call it a day, but at the end of a day we find ourselves trapped. We don't like to think about it, but it's true, and deep down we know it. It's the draining energy of living a routine life.

We are zombies sleepwalking through our awakening.

When we hear the word "awakening," we may find ourselves overwhelmed by visions of the heavens opening and thunderbolts of lightning (very, very frightening) coming down on us as we look out over the horizon and sweep our hand in a majestic motion over the landscape. Awakenings happen in small moments and with a gentle touch, but if we're buried up to our necks with endless routines, we will miss them.

What is an awakening? There are many definitions of awakening, but one describes it as "coming into existence or awareness."

Awakenings are like whispers from the Universe trying to get our attention.

These awakenings are meant to be a wakeup call in our lives, showing us that there is more to life than punching an imaginary time clock. Behind the curtain of routines lies a world that perhaps we should explore. Who knows what discoveries or journeys we will embark on?

Feeling trapped in a routine-driven life is like suffocation and not being able to breathe. It's a long, endless journey with no clear destination in mind, much less in sight. We can apply a single word to the routine-driven life, but it's a daunting concept: change.

Change is the enemy of routine because it calls for courage, faith, and strength.

Routine worships at the altar of mediocrity, whereas change calls us to not enter the church of average and adequate but to try different pathways to a new and better life. We can change the order in which we do things. Instead of going to get our coffee first thing in the morning, make it the second or third thing. It seems very simple, but it works, creating space for new experiences and clean energy. We might meet people we would never have met if we had not shed the cloak of a routine-driven life.

Change begins slowly, much like turning on a dimmer switch, and as we experience things that previously were not part of our routine, the light gets brighter and brighter, much like dawn gradually wakes us up. This is how an awakening happens because the Universe is not an on/off switch. Change the order of things; do some things you've never done before; meet new people; experience different things; and do the unexpected. Break away from societal expectations and start living. Nothing is wrong with starting a new routine.

Hidden Alignments

The word "universe" has many definitions and serves many purposes. The physical universe comprises planets, stars, galaxies, and dark matter, among other elements. The word "physical" in the above definition loosely refers to dark matter, as it is a hypothetical concept. Normally, when we think of the universe that I just described, we look up towards the heavens. The metaphysical or spiritual Universe is above us, around us, and consists of many realms, including the spirit side of life. These realms include our loved ones, spiritual beings, angels, ascended masters, spirit guides, heaven, light, dimensions of time and space, energy, frequencies, and vibrations (the last three also apply to the physical universe). Of course, our Creator, whom some refer to as God, is present in this realm as well as any other universe or realm that exists and has ever existed.

Our soul plan consists of a series of spiritual alignments that help keep our energy on the right path.

Think of it this way: We go into a tire store to get an alignment so that we can drive safely and keep on the road to arrive at our destination. The analogy above bears a striking resemblance to the previously described Universe. The Universe is the tire store, and whether we realize it or not, our energy drives our soul plan (the car) into the tire shop to get an alignment. This is so we can get back on the right path in life and keep manifesting our true destiny. There are no coincidences in life, only alignments.

Coincidences are nothing more than the Universe's alignments hiding underneath.

We have free will to do as we please, which includes recognizing the signs that we previously believed to be coincidences, to now be the Universe's way of aligning our spiritual selves to go forward on our path towards our mission and purpose. We also have free will to ignore those signs and go on different paths that sometimes do not end well. This is how we learn.

The Universe does not test us but lays out in front of us lessons to, hopefully, be learned.

It is a classroom full of knowledge. Nobody is putting us through hard times to teach us a lesson, but the hard times do offer many lessons. The lessons we learn or don't learn are based on decisions we make or do not make.

The Universe is not pulling our strings but pulling us to be good students in life's classroom.

The Universe is not so much a puppet master but a headmaster imparting wisdom upon us. If we believe in our ability to manifest our own destiny, then we need to make sure we take responsibility for our actions, both positive and negative. Lessons, alignments, and spirituality are there in front of us. We need to use our five senses to locate our sixth—we all have that ability.

The "Need To" Tribe

There is a tribe that at one point we all belonged to and still may belong to. That tribe is known as the Need to Tribe (NTT). This tribe dwells in the land of intentions. There is more information on that land in this book. The NT tribe (Need To) for the most part means well. The members of this tribe feel they have a certain calling—to give advice, counsel, direction, and so on—to assist others. In doing so they say "you need to" often. This intervention may be based on several factors, such as they just want to help, or they just want to tell people what to do.

They see themselves as someone who could correct the person's situation or, worse, fix the person. They have several lines that they use to put the person on a better path. One of the lines that they love is, "You need to let go" or "You need to let that go." We've all heard it and have all said it. There is a challenge, however, with this tribe's approach. "You need to" is not advice, counsel, or even a suggestion. The "You need to" statement can be seen by some as a direct order, plain and simple.

To be honest, it can also be seen as a controlling statement. Again, not all the time and not all the members of the tribe fall into that group.

When we say to someone "you need to," it's the same as pointing a finger. There's a huge difference between talking to someone and talking with someone.

Talking to someone is a lecture; talking with someone is a conversation.

When we talk to someone, it's a one-way street with a dead end. Talking with someone opens the door to dialogue, which leads to a conversation. This begs the thought that comes to us when we're sitting across the table from a member of the NTT: "Why are they trying to fix me? I didn't ask for this. I just wanted someone to listen to me." As members of the NTT, we are all well intended but not very good at listening. We must learn to pause and give the person we're trying to help some space.

When we let others come to their own conclusions, it is when awakening happens, not when we attempt to steer them down the need-to path. The space may prompt them to ask for advice and counsel, so the "you need to" statement will not be necessary. Do others need us to listen to them? Yes, as long as we give them room to breathe.

Trinity of the Soul

There are endless conversations about the soul and its purpose. Even if we are not in a spiritual mindset, there is little debate about the existence of our soul. Some may consider the heart the soul of our body; others consider our entire being our soul. In the current consciousness movement, and for those with a spiritual nature, the soul is much more.

For argument's sake, let's make a broad assumption that there are three "selves" to the soul. The False, the True, and the Higher Self. There are different perceptions about this, so just keep an open mind. These three selves have different properties that make them unique in their relationship to us. There are also two other selves mentioned in this book, the Old Self and the Shadow Self.

*The False and the True selves are philosophical, while the Higher Self is metaphysical.*_

FALSE SELF. This self is mentioned by many scholars, philosophers, and mystics as an example of what we are not. This part of our soul is occupied by roles that we play, facades that we put, as well as borders and boundaries designed to keep people out and to keep thoughts, words, and actions from becoming part of our True Self.

The False Self, while not always negative in nature, hides us from realizing our potential as members of a functioning society and as a member of the spiritual world. The False Self often disguises itself as a Shadow Self, attempting to cross over and attach itself to the True Self in order to present itself to the world as who we really are.

TRUE SELF. This is who we really are, stripped of the roles, rules, and regulations that society places upon us. This part of our soul deals with emotions, feelings, insight, and intuition, which goes down to the core of our being, revealing what kind of person we are to the world. The True Self doesn't hide and pretends to be something that it's not. By continuing to improve ourselves with good choices and helping others on their path, the True Self blossoms and overcomes the False Self so that a clear picture is shown to everyone around us. We all have a False Self, but it's up to us to determine how large a part in our lives we want it to play.

HIGHER SELF. It is the point of contact with the Creator (again, any name or label you want to place in the place of "Creator" works). Metaphysically, it's the main part of our soul that provides us with a 30,000-foot view of our lives, past, present, and future. Some equate the Higher Self to the seventh chakra, which is the white light on top of our head that ascends to a higher dimension. Others refer to it as a higher level of consciousness, but whatever we choose to describe it, we all have one. It's the guiding light and pathway to the other side, where wisdom, knowledge, love, peace, and understanding dwell in abundant supply.

Prayer, meditation, nature (anything that draws us closer to the Divine) help us on our path to higher dimensions, which many call heaven. We can all talk to our Higher Self just as we talk to a loved one who has passed. We make up who we are, philosophically and metaphysically. By recognizing these selves mentioned in this book, perhaps we will gain a deeper understanding of our spiritual identity.

Burying the Past

We all have the tendency to dig up the past every now and then. Sometimes we look back to see if there are any valuable lessons. I'm sure everyone can learn something by visiting the past. The key word in the above statement is visiting, not living in the past.

When we dig up the past, we become nothing more than grave robbers.

We could all have a lifetime of happiness, love, peace, and joy if not for walking back into the house of deeds that had gone wrong in the past. To be sure, there are good memories to look back on that make us smile, but we can't let go of the fact that in our lives we have made many mistakes on numerous occasions.

Admitting we're flawed is seen by some as a weakness, but it's really a sign of recognizing our identity—flawed but beautiful.

We all hear people tell us, "You need to let that go" when it comes to visiting the past. The problem is that no one has ever walked our path. Indeed, everyone has their own path to experience. The past offers numerous paths that, if we wander too far and for too long, can lead us to become captive to old habits, both good and bad.

Also, we must acknowledge that everyone, including ourselves, has experienced pain in the past. We all need to remind ourselves that the past, which wasn't so good, was there to teach us lessons. Again, let's all learn from these lessons, move forward, and never look back. After all, we are made to experience the present moment.

If we're going to bury the past, remember to throw away the shovel.

CHAPTER FIVE

MINDFULNESS

"The past has no power over the present moment."

—Eckhart Tolle

OVERVIEW

Mindfulness in this chapter explores the awareness of saying goodbye, the last word, judgments, validations, coincidences, guardrails, and the many paths we find ourselves on. Mindfulness is calling us to recognize inside and outside everything that is below us, within us, and above us.

The Final Bow

Towards the end of our physical existence on earth, several things start to happen as we take a final bow and say goodbye to hopefully a good life.

The last breath of our physical becomes the first breath of our spiritual.

We breathe out everything physical that was left behind on the physical plane and breathe in the energy, frequency, and vibrations of the Spirit world. One thing that connects all of us, whether we like it or not, is that we have a first breath when we are born and a last breath when we pass. What we do with this lifetime in between those breaths is what matters.

There are people, of course, who believe differently when it comes to the subject of a spiritual body. There are people who do not believe in the afterlife and feel that this is it. Nothing else matters. They see the reality of a physical body living and dying. They believe in the here and now, not what is to come, spiritual or otherwise. They are the non-believers who believe in what they see and touch.

Then there's the "camp" of individuals who strongly believe in the afterlife and what is to come. They are believers who insist that this physical life is just a prelude to something greater than themselves. They believe in what they cannot see (to some extent) or touch.

Both camps hold extreme ideologies. The conviction that exists within non-believers focuses on physical aspects of their lives. The distant future for them is mostly irrelevant. To say that they are firmly grounded is an understatement. They are so grounded in the earth that they can only see at eye level. To them, the physical world is real, and the spirit world is an illusion. To believers, it's the opposite. We're talking about a belief system, so there is no need to get worked up.

The believers also have their own convictions. This group believes everything revolves around something beyond physical life. They are solely focused on the hereafter and not the here and now. They are grounded, but barely. They are hanging on to their tiptoes as their heads float among the clouds. Again, these are certain groups. These descriptions do not apply to most people. The question is how to get non-believers to raise their gaze to see things that aren't there and have faith that there is something greater than us that awaits when we pass, and how to get believers to lower their gaze so that they focus their energy on this earth and this dimension we're in. How do we do this? Simple…we don't.

It's not our job, if you will, to "save" someone from themselves. Those who do not believe are just as good people as those who do believe. There is just a difference in belief system, although it's a good-sized belief system. We show them what it means to us to believe in the afterlife. No lectures or sermons; no badgering them for a home visit so that we can have them see the error of their ways. We pray, give them space, and give them time, and then that's it. Information can become knowledge if applied correctly.

One More Thing

When was the last time we had to get the last word in? We couldn't wait to tell someone or somebody exactly what they needed to hear, or so we thought. Getting in the last word leaves a lasting impression for the wrong reason. Once again, we're talking about energy—in this case, negative energy. "One more thing" never ends a conversation; instead, the conversation can potentially turn into confrontation depending on the situation.

One more thing, or the last word, leads to a multitude of things that allows the negative energy strand to continue between participants in the conversation. Not having the last word is the only way to break this continuous thread of one-upmanship.

We don't need to walk away from someone and then turn around and say, "And one more thing." I'm sure we have witnessed an argument in which one of the gladiators won't fight back. Soon thereafter, the person who wanted to continue the verbal assault is filled with anger and rage because the negative energy was not received by the person who walked away. The negative energy has consumed the instigator because it has nowhere else to go. They have now entered the house of anger and are breathing in the air.

Breathing life into anger gives birth to bitterness.

If we cannot be silent and have to say something, consider saying, "You may have a point," and then walk away. Don't linger or wait for a response because that invites more negative energy. If more people took this action, we could prevent situations from "coming to a head." Our words can possess healing energy, and they can also possess hurtful energy.

Silence is sometimes the most profound and effective way to de-escalate a conversation that has confrontation brewing beneath the surface. Let's all pause before we decide to talk. We're not called to talk all the time, as silence truly is golden. Let others talk. They might find common ground by themselves.

Long Goodbye

The moment we are born, we begin a (hopefully) long journey of goodbyes. I understand that we're meeting people all our lives, but at the same time, we're also saying goodbye. There is a lot of emphasis on meeting new people, introducing ourselves to others, and joining like-minded social groups and communities, and that's all good. However, it's important to realize that we are saying goodbye the minute we say hello. When we make the connections with anyone, let's make sure we're using our God-given energy to make the space we occupy a positive place for conversations and relationships.

For others to come into our energy, even if their energy doesn't exactly align with ours, we should always strive to leave no one behind, especially those whom we might have met and forgotten about a long time ago.

Experts suggest that about 80% of the people we meet may never be seen again.

During the day today, we encountered many people on the internet, telephone, cell phone, FaceTime, traffic, over lunch, during a meeting, etc., that we may not see again. Some of these encounters were brief, others were long, but regardless of the duration of the encounter, there was a reason you and the other person or people shared a moment. You may never know the reason for the encounter, but energy was present, hopefully in a good way. This and other encounters we experience daily are sometimes the only opportunity to share a moment in the form of thoughts, words, action, deeds, and so on. Before we say goodbye, let's leave them with a kind word or two that they might need to move them forward on their day.

Judgement Day

It's hard not to judge. It's a bottomless pit that we can all fall into, and if we aren't careful, we will stay there. We want to judge—not observe or listen, but judge how people act, dress, walk, talk, weigh, parent their kids, wear their hair, work, make money—you get the idea. Underneath it all, judging becomes our default setting when we interact with people. If we can group things that people do or don't do that fit into descriptions that we understand and agree with, then all will be right with the world.

So much energy is spent on attempting to do the above that it's a wonder we get any rest. Again, why do we do that? What do we care about what people look like, talk like, act like, dress like, and so on? If what others do makes them happy and content, then so be it. The adage of "live and let live" should still resonate today, but we would be hard-pressed to look around and witness this on display.

Let them live the way they want to live, not the way we want them to live. It's their life, and it's time we stopped judging other people for being them. It's ok that they're different, because so are we.

Perhaps we should change "Live and Let Live" to "Love and Let Love."

When we interact with others, we should remember that they are someone's father, mother, daughter, son, aunt, uncle, grandfather, grandmother, grandson, granddaughter, nephew, niece, close friend, etc. They deserve, as we all do, to live their lives in their own way as far as we are concerned. Unfortunately, others will frequently judge them for who they are and what they do. Let's avoid adding our names to the numerous judges they will face.

Allowing people to evolve by giving them space to breathe and live their lives the way they want is the best we can offer them.

Veil of Validations

Validations…they surround us like a faint heartbeat that gets louder and louder any time we reach out when we feel we need a boost. Every time we get on social media, we have this desire to make ourselves known to others and the world. Don't get me wrong, we all need them at crucial times in our lives. "You're great!" "You're wonderful!"

Validations are like a GPS when we feel lost. We just need a course correction. However, we don't need validations every minute, every day of our lives. We need to use our God-given gifts to give ourselves some space to discover and explore life. This constant desire for validation uncovers what's behind the veil. Behind this veil is the need to feel relevant, important, and wanted, so people will not forget about us. It's like high school all over again.

It could be a simple cry for help, which we need to be on the lookout for. It could be just reaching out innocently to stay in touch with others. Once the veil of validations is parted, there appear to be several reasons we need validation in our lives, but one thing seems to be at the core of every validation: the need to feel relevant. Not feeling relevant in life is not feeling, period. Relevance is not the same as not feeling important, but it does border on feeling left out. It's as if we don't matter in life or that nobody wants us. Sometimes the loneliness that people feel and the silence that surrounds the disenfranchised, the marginalized, the left-behind group, etc., must be deafening.

These folks are desperately waving their hands from the back of the room, saying, "Don't forget about me!" Or the young boy or girl hoping and praying with their hands so tightly it hurts, saying, "Please pick me. I'm somebody, and I want to belong."

I wonder how long that sticks with people. To say "pull yourself up from your bootstraps" falls on deaf ears. Some people feel they are naked, literally and symbolically, with no clothes on, much less bootstraps. The bootstraps in this scenario are inside a person's soul, and for the soul to start pulling, there must be a meeting between mind, body, and spirit where everyone is on page to conclude that we are worthy… plain and simple.

The opportunity is there because we are all worth it in the eyes of God. Be confident that our lives are validated just by being who we are. "Be still and know that I am God."

The most important word in that equation is BE. That's all we can do.

Guardrails

When we go through a school zone, there are speed bumps to slow us down, so we are not going too fast. It's for our own safety and for the safety of others. When we go through a construction zone, we must navigate barricades (by Bob) and go slow so as not to destroy property or hurt anyone, especially ourselves. When we drive on roads that might be unsafe, there are detours to steer us away from danger.

I know what you're thinking. The next line is going to be "Life is like that!" Well, that's true… blockades, re-directions, potholes, drivers with no sense of direction or safety for themselves and others… they're all on our journeys throughout life. I would like to draw attention to another item, and that is the scenario above regarding the guardrails that protect us from dangers of all shapes and sizes.

Who or what are the guardrails in our lives?

I'm speaking of guardrails that prevent us from making huge mistakes, wrong decisions, going in the wrong direction, etc. I'm talking about listening to your inner voice to safeguard your decision-making.

Our inner voice speaks the language of our soul.

While we're focusing on our soul, what about the people around us who are using their intuition to help us? Instead of dismissing those folks as interfering, let's welcome them as they put up signs over potholes in our lives to help us navigate around the dangers that lie ahead. Sometimes we are guardrails, providing clarity, comfort, and closure to those around us. Am I a guardrail to my friends and family? Am I doing a good job of helping those who need it? Do I set up guardrails for myself so that I don't lose sight of who I am and where I am?

Widen the Path (but Narrow the Lane)

Sometimes our life goes on a path that we least expect it to. It's amazing the impact driving on a wide road gives us—freedom, space, room to breathe, and the thrill of letting it rip, pointing its nose down the highway and letting the horses within the hood of the car loose. On a wide path, we can experience the same sense of freedom. But no matter how big, large, or wide the path is, we have to remain in our lane. If we don't, we invite possible danger or chaos when crossing lanes or diverting ourselves from our goal of arriving at our destination.

When we discover the gifts that the Universe has given us, we sometimes look over in the other lanes to see what gifts God has given others. We may start to wonder why we don't have those gifts, almost like admiring with jealousy the nice, shiny car or truck that is in the lane next to us. With all the gifts that all those shiny, new, beautiful cars have, we start to wonder what it would be like to possess such gifts. So we start to cross over into other lanes, sometimes dangerously.

The Universe tells us daily to stay in our lane, no matter how narrow it is. There will be time to explore those other lanes in the path, but for now, work on our gifts until we feel a tap on the shoulder from the Universe that says, "It's time to switch lanes and discover something new that will enrich your life and others." We must have patience with our gifts.

Patience is the cloak that is waiting to cover humanity.

The lessons that patience teaches are valuable but challenging, as time can either be a blessing or a curse. We are people who covet ideas, emotions, feelings, energy, vibrations, conversations, and friendships, so patience is usually not our strongest trait. Let's not lose our patience while we're in our lane and look straight ahead until we get the sign from the Universe.

CHAPTER SIX

CONTEMPLATION

"Empty your mind, be formless, shapeless, like water."

—Bruce Lee

OVERVIEW

Contemplation evolves into many forms, images, and thoughts. Included in chapter six is karma, right from wrong, the afterlife, and deciding whether to jump or not. This chapter is the shortest in this book, but contemplation is no short or small matter. To contemplate means to think deeply at a subject matter for an extended period.

Looking at the above themes, I think most of us, if not all of us, would agree that these are deep topics to tackle. However, the Universe has confidence in us that we can decipher the various messages this chapter presents, and I share the same confidence.

Standing on the Edge

Sometimes we jump, and sometimes we hesitate. If we picture ourselves on the edge of a cliff, what will compel us to jump?

What or who are we afraid of?

What do we hope to find if we arrive at the conclusion of this decision?

What are we trying to run away from, or better yet, what is it that we think we're trying to run to?

The final decision we make (in that last impulse, a split second really) can change the course of our lives and that of many others, namely our family, friends, co-workers, associates, and even the clerk at the Starbucks drive-through… The list is endless.

If we believe we're all connected, then the result of our decision will resonate forever. It becomes our Big Bang moment that will resonate in the history books of the Universe.

What will be our decision?

How would we feel about the decision that we made?

Will the decision to jump or not, change anything?

What will change in the future as a result of our decision?

Are others able to make a similar decision?

No matter what we think this chapter is about, it serves its purpose if you can visualize standing on the edge of a cliff, taking a deep breath to go and see what awaits you. As we visualize and manifest this possible turning point in our lives, remember to think about what life was like or is like as you contemplate making the jump.

Also consider, one last time, before you make the decision, what life will be like if you make the jump. This chapter is about many things, but only you know what it means to you. It's as personal as any chapter in this book. When it comes to regrets, what, if any, is our exit strategy?

More importantly, do we even have one? If not, might it be time to contemplate and see what comes to the top?

Blame It on Karma

If I could get into the mindset of what the world refers to as "karma," here's what I believe about the numerous discussions and conversations surrounding it. Something happens to us that we think is without a doubt a grave injustice, and here comes the karma quote: "Karma is a bitch." Or "Karma will get them." There are three groups who seem to reference karma at will.

1. *The Revenge Seekers.* Karma is many things, but it's not revenge. Revenge is messy, dark, useless, and negative… The list is endless, but one thing revenge does is cast us into the sea of negativity, going down further and further under water as we plot even a minor act of revenge, until we get to the point where we can't break free and swim to the surface to distance ourselves away from the grip and mindset of making someone pay.

The energy surrounding revenge is negative, and the minute we get lured into its tentacles, we become engulfed in anger and no better than the person or people who “targeted” us in the first place.

2. *The Martyr Seekers.* This one will resonate with some of us: “Well, it’s my karmic life coming back to haunt me.” Translation: This person, like me, believes in past lives and therefore believes they’re doomed in this lifetime, no matter what they do, so they go about their daily routines blaming everything on something that happened in a previous lifetime.

There’s an element of truth in that thinking, but it’s an element that can be changed by a belief in manifesting our destiny. To accept this mindset of being suffocated by karma is to basically say, “I’m predestined to be miserable, a failure, a lost soul, and there’s nothing I can do about it.” We make a checklist of all the things that have gone wrong in our lives and chalk it up to “karmic life.” Excuses will not light a path in the right direction. We sweep it under the karmic rug, only to pull it out when we need an excuse to explain that the situations that we’re going through aren’t our fault. This means that we do not have free will to manifest our destiny.

So, what is karma? Karma has many explanations and means different things to different people, but, to me, the core of karma lies in enlightenment, not revenge; not an excuse as to why things aren't going right in our lives.

Karma is not revenge, nor a bitch.

3. *The Free Thinkers and Open-Minded.* It boils down to enlightenment. Karma is part of the universal classroom where we learn about previous lives and how to learn those lessons and apply them to our current lives. So, what happens to those who have wronged us?

They can learn those lessons from past lives and obtain enlightenment to help them in this lifetime, or they can ignore those lessons and take their chances. I prefer to be in group number three.

How, then, can we change our karmic life? Here are some thoughts.

- If we're swimming in negativity, change lanes.
- Decline all invitations to pity parties. (again)
- Something must be destroyed before creation takes place. Old habits and ways of thinking must cease to exist so that a new karmic life can be born.

- How we see others is how we should see ourselves. It all starts with us.
- Discover light even if surrounded by darkness.

Let's all be good students and learn what all our lives have taught us and will continue to teach us.

We can change the karmic course of our lives by thinking, believing, and using our behavior to manifest our destiny. If we believe that in the past we were a dark person, it's time to wipe the slate clean, break the trend of negativity, and start fresh with a renewed purpose to add positivity to this karmic life.

Blurred Lines

One of the earliest lessons we learn between one and three years of age is right from wrong. This is mainly a lesson on what not to do by hearing the word "no" or getting a slight slap on the wrist, among other actions designed to reinforce the "we don't do that" lesson. We as children then figure out, hopefully, that by doing the opposite or different (if it's good), we will be getting a reward such as a cookie or a hug from our mom or dad. This is achieved through constant reinforcement for doing good things. A slap on the wrist for bad behavior and a hug for good behavior.

A child is like the T-Rex in *Jurassic Park*, constantly testing the fence, looking for an opening that will result in a cookie or an opportunity to go on a rampage, create havoc, and cause mass destruction. But I digress. (Just kidding.)

Children make mistakes, and parents are there to correctly put them on the right path through constant reminders and reinforcement. Unfortunately, as we grow older, we cease to look right and wrong the same way as when we were children. The question is, how did the boxes of right and wrong open and spill into each other?

When did the lines of right and wrong become so blurred that they are unrecognizable?

We were supposed to work hard for companies until we retired. Nowadays, cutbacks and layoffs affecting people in their 30s, 40s, and 50s are the rule and not the exception. Somewhere, a corporate executive or a bean counter in an office decides to cut payroll with the stroke of a pen, all in the name of increasing the bottom line and delivering record profits for the privileged few. Someone figured out that to improve the bottom line, payroll had to be cut. Pulling the lever on payroll is the easiest and quickest way to save money and increase profits. It's the easiest decision, but it should be the hardest. Affecting people's lives in such a manner is devastating to families, communities, small businesses, and the individual.

In the past, such a thing would be big news when it happened. In today's environment, this is an everyday occurrence. It's no longer big news or even news at all. Yes, many companies, big and small, treat their employees as associates and give them great benefits, great wages, opportunities for growth, and plans for retirement.

I've had the pleasure of working for two companies that were very good to their people, and someone close to me was the head of a major corporation that did the right things constantly for their people, so it can be done. It should be done. I'm a big believer in capitalism and companies, both big and small. But it seems that great companies are few and far between in today's marketplace, because after all, what's more important than money?

Where is the trickle-down effect on everyone in the company? Again, many companies are great at this, but some… not so much. We justify such actions by thinking, "This is what I'm supposed to do." Have people in business, politics (don't get me started), entertainment, sports, etc., forgotten the golden rule? "Do unto others as you would have them do unto you."

We have a responsibility to do the right thing in life. Our childhood taught us that. But we blur the lines of right and wrong so that our justification makes sense to us. We convince ourselves we're doing the right thing. Whatever happened to letting our conscience be our guide?

Is it our conscience or our convictions that guide us in making decisions?

We don't tell the truth about people by gossiping behind their backs because they're "just white lies," and it won't hurt anyone because even though it's not true, it could be… There's the justification. We start rumors about people because they start rumors about us, so it's time for some payback. We take small things from our workplace because we feel like they owe it to us. We cheat on our taxes just a little because what's going to hurt? Besides, doesn't the government owe us? The lines of right and wrong are so blurred and close together that they seem to merge into one.

We've talked ourselves into justifying what is right and what is wrong.

It's our system of frontier justice that only we control. Children are not allowed in the frontier because they would tell us what we're doing is wrong, and deep down, we know we can't handle that. The lines are blurred because we saw society doing it, so we figured we would play along.

It's time to be a non-conformist and do the right thing in life. Our inner child implores us to get back to what it means to be a good citizen of this planet. It's overdue long. Let's pretend our loved ones, especially children, are looking over our shoulders when we're contemplating doing something that we know isn't right. Time to get reacquainted with the law of right and wrong.

What Did I Do?

We learn at a very early age that not everyone likes us, and sometimes, no matter what we do or how much we change or try to change, this person is not going to be our friend. Even worse is the situation where they take it to another level by imposing their will on us in the form of bullying or isolation. It could be the color of our skin, our clothes, the way we look, our face, the way we walk, how we laugh, what we believe in, what sports we play or don't play, what our hair looks like; the list is endless.

Even as we get older, some of these situations still drive us up a wall; why don't they like us? Here is the question that goes through our mind when presented with this dilemma. What did I do? When we were young, we learned from our parents, siblings, grandparents, uncles, aunts, and teachers at school what was acceptable to do and what wasn't. Our support system would constantly teach us what and what not to do. What I described above is an example of what some would consider a normal household.

Some people may read the above and reflect, "That is not how I grew up." These are the folks who may have grown up in abusive, single-parent households in crime-ridden or poor neighborhoods. If you were told the only time to get down on the floor wasn't to read a book or listen to a story but to avoid possibly getting shot by someone driving by, then there was no time to reflect on why people may not like us.

Sometimes we ponder for a moment why crime rates are high among certain groups, until we begin to understand what some members of those groups have learned: there is no right and wrong, only survival or non-survival.

We've got to embrace and work with those (resource-wise) who continue to be marginalized by an ignorant society. This scenario should answer the question, "Didn't they learn right from wrong growing up?" No, they were too busy trying to figure out where the next meal was coming from. They need us to help them learn this important lesson before it's too late, and that lesson is that they didn't do anything wrong. For those of us who had somewhat of a support system to help teach us right from wrong, there's a question again that needs to be asked: When and where have the lines of right and wrong become blurred?

The more the lines are blurred and faded, the more difficult it is to see them as we grow older and further away from our inner child remembering what is right and what isn't.

Here are some questions that we might ask ourselves when people don't like us and some answers that might offer some clarity.

What did I do? Maybe it was a mistake, maybe something intentional, maybe nothing at all. We may never know, but it may be best to move on before the question consumes us to the point where we can no longer tolerate it.

Can I fix it? Always make the effort so we can say we gave it our best. Who knows; it might be fixable or not, but we can pray for the best possible outcome.

Chance for reconciliation of some sort?

You never know when time will work. Send positive energy to the situation and keep the door cracked in case someone wants to come back into our life. Now, let's reverse this scenario. There are people we don't like; we can't put our finger on why we don't like them other than the fact that we just don't. It doesn't matter what they do to make up for it or try to fix it; according to us, it won't matter. We just don't like them. If we listen closely, we can hear them thinking, "What did I do? Can I fix it? Will we ever be friends again?"

What do we do?

Well, it seems to me that being the nicest person we can be is a major first step. This at least sets the table for a possible reunion or reconciliation of some sort. So, what if they say no? We're doing all we can. Then we move on and wish them well.

Making our grudges light makes it easier to let go of them.

Are we doing the right or wrong things in life? Our inner child knows.

The Afterlife, Part I

The existence of heaven and hell has been debated for centuries and undoubtedly will be debated for the rest of eternity. Is the existence of heaven and hell a question that can be answered? There are over 3,000 religions in the world and most of them believe in an existence beyond the physical body. First, is there an afterlife? Everything I've seen, heard and experienced tells me yes, and this goes beyond conventional, structured religion. The proof is overwhelming among those who have experienced near-death experiences.

The next question might be, is this heaven and hell or different levels of consciousness? Consciousness is one of the few things that science cannot explain or find. There is artificial intelligence, but there isn't artificial consciousness because the consciousness and soul cannot be dissected in a laboratory. Lately, advancements in afterlife technology have included measuring soundwaves, energy, tapping into a consciousness stream, etc. When someone passes, they give us a small peek into the other side. Near-death experiences have blown the doors off the skeptic community with numerous people accurately reciting what they felt when they crossed over.

These sensations are almost identical, from the tunnel of light to sounds, colors, and music to the heavenly voices of people to being able to repeat verbatim conversations that doctors, surgeons, and nurses had while trying to save that person's life. They can go through the surgery step by step while they are unconscious with remarkable detail. There is also the life review that numerous people have reported. To begin the task of trying to understand the possible existence of heaven or hell, the admittance of not being able to fully come to grips with the notion that there are things that we cannot explain or offer a defense of is a step in the right direction. To admit that there is "something out there" means we've taken a huge first step.

Let's go back to NDEs. While it is true that most people who have crossed over have felt and experienced a positive wave of energy, there are those whose NDE was anything but a pleasurable experience. Some have reported a "hellish" experience with demons and the likec. They describe a horrifying place and existence for those folks who are there. So, there you go.

People who have crossed over and come back are the people worth listening to. If we believe in certain religious beliefs, then we must believe that there is this entity of evil personified, in the lower realms or dimensions, that some refer to as hell. But if you follow the golden rule, "Do unto others as you would have them do unto you," and help your neighbor, no matter what kind of person they are, then you're truly making a positive difference in the world, and let's let that be the last word. Never forget that the continuity of life gives us hope.

The Afterlife, Part II

This chapter is for all who believe that this life may not be all there is to living but may feel labels such as specific religions, heaven, hell, etc., are not for them. This chapter will also look at Jesus as a defining figure in the history of the world.

We may ask ourselves, "I believe there's something beyond my five senses, but I'm not sure what it is or what to call it." Some people refer to this as "the other side." On this other side that people occasionally think about, talk about, debate, or just ignore, it does raise the question: is there another side and what is it actually?

In another chapter we explore Heaven and Hell, but this is a no-labels approach to the realms and dimensions beyond our five senses. We may ask ourselves the following questions:

- What is it?
- How do we get there?
- Do we have to die to experience it?
- Is the afterlife in this other side?
- Is it the stars and the Universe?
- Is it "dark matter" that makes up a huge percentage of the Universe?
- Is it up in the clouds like Heaven?

If we can keep an open mind and not let religion get in the way of our thoughts, then think about the possibilities of beyond the physical world and beyond our five senses.

Clairvoyants and mediums can connect with loved ones with little or no previous information in amazing detail, just as a psychic can pick up energy of thoughts and future events with uncanny descriptions. All this with the belief that the creator knows all. There's no explanation for that other than the information coming from outside our five senses: in other words, the other side. We don't know everything, but hopefully we can start to gain more knowledge about the unknown. Trust me when I say this: it's never too late. Just keep an open mind.

If your mind is open to things unseen, then the unknown starts to come into focus.

Keep your mind open to all possibilities beyond what we deem normal… You don't have to embrace it; just give it a little hug every now and then, and you will realize it.

Let's discuss a prominent figure who not only resides in the afterlife but also here on earth in the hearts and minds of many. I'm speaking of the man called Jesus.

When it comes to the topic of Jesus, there are thousands of opinions as to who or what this man, this deity, this mystery is or was. Everyone has an opinion on Jesus, some stronger than others, but make no mistake about it: whether you're a believer or not, everyone at some point in their life has had or will have a conversation about "him."

The man is one of the most inspirational, motivational, sacred, and yet at the same time, polarizing figures of all time. Jesus isn't owned by Christianity. Many religions revere and acknowledge, maybe not in the same manner or light, but they do recognize the impact he has had on the world.

Even some of the newer churches, such as the metaphysical and non-denominational churches, give special homage to this man and other enlightened and ascended ones who are in the afterlife. Jesus transcends religion and is mentioned in metaphysical practices as an ascended master.

Even if some do not recognize him as the son of God, he is regarded as a man of peace, preaching against violence. His parables, or stories, give us hope for the future, teach peace, and to show us the error of our ways. This is how he taught, giving us lessons that would hold up for centuries to come.

He opposed the hypocritical use of power by church leaders. He preached about grace and mercy, not revenge and violence. He reached out to children as a symbol of innocence and love.

Jesus does transcend across many religions, but the one that he is associated with is Christianity, and therein lies a challenge. Christianity claims Jesus as its own, but he was Jewish. Christianity wants to keep him in the Bible, so only they can praise and worship him.

If you don't fall in lockstep with Christianity and are not saved, you are deemed a heathen or an outsider. Nothing could be further from the truth. Jesus never turned anyone away. He welcomed everybody and talked about loving our neighbor more than once in the Bible.

So, who are those neighbors that Jesus wants us to love? Our neighbors include individuals who identify as atheists, agnostics, Christians, Muslims, Hindus, and Jews; individuals who identify as straight, gay, bisexual, lesbians, and transsexuals; individuals who are brown, black, yellow, white, and orange; individuals who identify as male, female, or non-binary; Native Americans; and individuals who belong to any of the more than three thousand religions that make up the world.

You don't have to follow a certain religion to talk to Jesus. He is always there to listen.

If you're comfortable with not knowing or wondering what's out there, that's fine and good. You do you. But on the other hand, if you stop and pause for a moment, look up, look around, and say to yourself, "I wonder?" ... Welcome aboard.

CHAPTER SEVEN

THOUGHTS

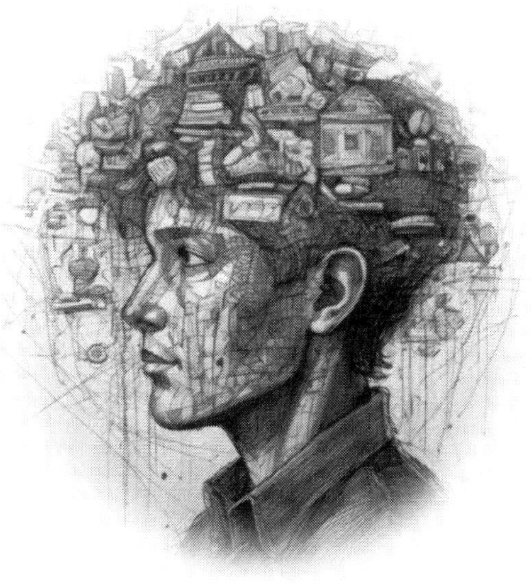

"If everybody is thinking alike, then somebody isn't thinking."

—George S. Patton

OVERVIEW

Consider subjects like perfection, religion, safety, church, brokenness, and metaphysics, and you'll see why this chapter's title is "Thoughts." These subjects call us to think about things differently by shining a light that challenges us all to not accept the status quo or go with conventional wisdom. As Spirit once told me: "People talk of conventional wisdom; I am wisdom." Let's all become enlightened and use our wisdom to look at things in a different light.

What Color Is Perfection?

Who decides what perfection is? How does it look? What are the characteristics and traits? How can we spot perfection when we see it? If we're not in that box of perfection, then how do we get there? It seems a bit surreal to me that we humans, who are flawed, are the ones to have conjured up in our minds what perfection is. An imperfect human race will offer up a definition of something that nobody is and never will be. Our minds are limited, and we're simply not wired to perceive what perfection is, mainly because it doesn't exist and has never existed.

Why chase something that is unobtainable?

As the old saying goes, "Nobody's perfect," and that's because no one is. We're all flawed, and therein lies the grace and beauty of who we are as people. There's no need to strive for something that cannot be defined. Pursuing something that cannot even be accurately defined is insanity. While it is true the color of perfection does not exist, neither does perfection, and we're wasting our time trying to define it, much less explain it.

Religion's Trap Door

"Just work on your fundamentals, and they will get you where you need to be." "Perfect the fundamentals and go from there." We've heard this throughout our lives. Why do I equate the term or word "fundamentals" with the title of this chapter? Because in the statements above, there's no mention of what to do once you've perfected the fundamentals. Go from there? Where? A better term (for me anyway) is *foundation.*

Every organization, movement, religion, political process, and sports team begins with a fundamental foundational idea, which serves as a framework for further development. The challenge, especially in religion, is that they don't seem to have forward vision in which to keep expanding and building upon and exploring the mindset of the core idea of the foundation.

Looking at the above statement "Perfect the fundamentals and go from there." This is a true statement, except some religions never "go from there." Traditions keep them rooted in their current place. But how do traditions get started? Could it be time to create new traditions in religion, but on solid ground from the fundamental foundation on which the idea was built upon?

Unfortunately, they just keep building the same idea because they are stuck in the cement of the foundation. Try this for a visualization of what I'm talking about. Since we're talking about religion, let's use it as an example. If we are to construct a metaphorical house of religion, we must first clear the land for its construction. Pour concrete and lay down the slab or foundation of the house. Put up walls, with spaces for windows. Put it on the roof to keep the weather from affecting the inside. Obviously, there's a lot more to be done, but unfortunately, this is where religion stops. They don't go beyond the four walls of a fundamental house. There's no plumbing, electricity, decorations, or furniture, and no way to express ourselves within the confines of the religion.

There's also no driveway or doors to go outside because mainstream religion doesn't want you to leave.

Religion wants us to stay in that house and not seek other opportunities for avenues of spiritual growth. It's ok to peek outside the window occasionally, but shame on whoever wants to wander across the street to check out another house of worship, especially if it's a "spiritual" place not affiliated with any specific religion.

The house of religion may hang a sign above the door that reads "ALL ARE WELCOME," but we know that isn't always the case. Let's ask ourselves this question: Have you ever seen a religious fanatic? We may have heard of and possibly even seen religious fanatics, but have we ever encountered or witnessed a spiritual fanatic? This should tell us a lot. Don't get me wrong; I loved my Methodist upbringing, and I love my Catholic religion. A religious foundation is a great starting point to build upon, and I highly recommend it, but to complete the spiritual vision, the rest is up to us. We should all consider starting a new chapter of welcoming everybody with our thoughts, our actions, and our prayers.

Inside the Safe House

The obvious purpose of a safe house is to keep us safe. The espionage world defines it as a place in another country where you can conduct business in an "undercover" or covert environment without detection. However, a safe house serves as a sanctuary for individuals who have experienced abuse, abandonment, or addiction struggles, serving as a place for recovery, relaxation, rehabilitation, and regaining confidence.

Eventually we must leave the secure structure and go outside.

Now, some people would say that inside this structure, it's as real as it gets. You experience a sense of safety and security, a sense of isolation from the world's negativity, yet venturing outside could potentially expose you to danger.

There is another safe house that is not a physical structure but a state of mind that most of us, if not all of us, occupy at certain times in our lives. This safe house is more metaphysical in nature because it does have energy, or at least as much energy as we give it. I'm talking about our mindset to play it safe. Some of us view this mindset as a short stay while others look at staying in the house for a long period of time, maybe for an entire life.

We don't take a risk; we don't step outside of our comfort zone to see what possibilities await us, to have a better future for ourselves and our family, to help those who need it and those that don't need it, to explore, to navigate, to discover, to see what we've missed, and to see what we can gain in knowledge and grace—the list is endless.

If we choose to take a risk, even a calculated one, we won't feel unsafe, even if we fail. What if we're wrong? What if this is a trap for me to experience humiliation? It's like we're in solitary confinement, but the door is wide open. Why do we play it safe? It could be past decisions about stepping out and letting our voice be heard. It didn't turn out well, so we say to ourselves, "Not going to do that again."

Yes, sometimes we learn to not repeat mistakes, but were they mistakes? And, if so, what's stopping us from applying what we learned in the first place and "making another run at" trying again but from a different angle?

By constantly playing it safe, we will effectively minimize the pain of being hurt, rejected, laughed at, etc. The key to getting out of the safehouse is to unlock the door inside that contains our dreams, walk out the front door, and breathe in the new life that awaits us and that we so richly deserve. Carry those dreams and never look back. When did playing it safe ever work out? Take a chance!

One Size Fits All

Every now and then, we look around to see that most, if not all, people seem to fit into life, except for us. We try as hard as we can to fit into life like others, but we always seem to fall short. Oh sure, we try the "just be yourself" strategy, but even that somehow doesn't do the trick, mainly because we're trying to be ourselves, but with one eye open to others around us to see if it's working. "Are we going to get in that group? That group looks good. It would be nice to fit into that." We're trying to be ourselves to fit it, and we know in the back of our minds, it's never going to work.

Instead of fitting into life, have life fit into you.

Maybe we want to be adopted and, therefore, included with those people or groups of people that we look at from afar and have admired for so long. Why do we admire them? That person and those groups? It's like we're in high school trying to fit into the popular group or crowd. After high school, many of the popular people struggle getting through life because the popular crowd disperses, and everyone goes their separate ways. The biggest, most important lesson in life also happens to be the one we all forget every day of our lives: that we're made in the image and likeness of the Creator, and to think less of ourselves is contrary to what the Universe wants for us. To live our lives and serve our purpose and meaning means that there are going to be times in which we just don't fit in. It's not the end of the world, and no one's legs or arms are going to fall off. It simply means we haven't found our tribe yet, but with each group that we don't seem to fit in with, we're one step closer to finding our sacred circle or group that we're destined to be with.

When we're busy trying to fit into life, we start to allow it to define our identity instead of us. We've all met people with whom we just had that "vibe" that we felt somehow made us uncomfortable even though we couldn't put our finger on it. I'm not talking about someone who does give off energy that says this person is not a good person. That's a different kind of discomfort. What I'm talking about are nice people, but maybe not our kind of people.

Could it be that our energy is creating an uncomfortable environment for others to settle in? Once we step away from trying to blend in with certain groups of people, our energy starts to create new space for the right people to use their energy to seek like-minded energies.

Over time, our energies will find others, even if it's only a temporary bond. By using our energies, we will find like-minded people to share our sacred space with. We will also find people who aren't like-minded. Who knows what impact we may have on them and what impact they may have on us? No time like the present.

Church of the Broken

The first time I went to an AA meeting, I was blown away. What I learned very quickly was that everything that is said and discussed in an AA meeting stays within its confines and is not to be discussed after the meeting ends. This is understandable, of course, because of the nature of alcoholism and other addictions that are related in some way.

The stories and testimonials that I have now heard and witnessed are nothing short of inspiring and give me hope for the future. These are people who have hit rock bottom and stayed there for a period, only to admit that they were powerless and needed a higher power to help save them.

This is what I call the "church of the broken," not to be confused with the "broken church." They have, in some cases, experienced lows and very few highs. Broken marriages, families shattered, dreams unrealized, incarceration, DUIs, death, drugs, destruction of property, suicide attempts, abuse—the list is endless. Some of them were atheists and either didn't believe in a God or thought, at least, if there is a God, "He's abandoned me and I'm all alone." "No one cares about me." "No one cares whether I live or die." "I've lost everything." "I have nothing, I have no value, and my life means nothing."

Then, by the grace of God, they somehow find their way into an AA room and meet people from all walks of life who are just as broken as they are, even more so. When they are surrounded by those who have been through what they've been through and then some, they have a sense of belonging. When they feel like they've found their tribe, they feel like they're no longer fighting a fight. When there's a devastating illness, such as alcoholism, there's a bond of blood to be shared. When they feel that they're part of a shared journey with others, their attitude changes.

I haven't mentioned religion mainly because it doesn't factor into most of the AA situations, at least in the beginning. Don't get me wrong; I love my Catholic religion, but rarely have I heard any religion, regardless of denomination, mentioned in these meetings. This is because the folks at AA didn't start out seeking religion; in fact, they didn't start out admitting the one thing none of us ever want to admit... that we're powerless. To get down on our metaphorical knees and say, to whomever is listening, that we're powerless to move forward with our lives.

We're powerless to stop hurting ourselves and those around us, especially those that we love and those that love us. This is a defining moment, a stark reminder that if we don't get help soon, our next step might be our last.

Admitting we're powerless and reaching out to a higher power might be what we all need from time to time. That higher power is always there. We're not bulletproof; we're flesh and blood, and at certain times in our lives, we are completely powerless, whether we want to admit it or not. In those moments, if we admit in some way that we don't have the power, the strength, the energy, or the courage to carry on, please know in those moments the higher power was listening and that you never were powerless and you never will be. He will always be listening.

Reading the Room

We've seen this scene played out time and time again whereby we're engaged in a conversation with someone, and it's becoming or has become clear that the person is saying things that offend us. Not by swearing or anything like that, but by ignoring simple aspects of conversation by being respectful and sensitive to the other person and what they may be going through. At this point, we may conclude that it's us; until someone else joins the conversation and the same thing happens to them.

What causes this? A bigger question is whether the people doing this are just being cruel or not aware of what they're doing. Several different answers are available here, but the scenario fits the description of what some call "reading the room" or, as in the case above, failure to read the room. What does reading the room mean?

Reading the room means picking up the sensitivity of people's energies, individually or in a group.

Empaths have no problem reading a room because they are sensitive to people's energies, mainly emotions and feelings. Reading the room means we must keep our emotions and feelings in check when we're engaged with someone or a group.

This will allow their emotions and feelings to flourish by giving them space. When we struggle to read the room, we lose our sensitivity to what the person is experiencing or has experienced. This is (also) called emotional intelligence. Emotional intelligence is a "condition" in which individuals with high emotional intelligence recognize the impact of their words and actions on others. Lack of emotional intelligence is, of course, the opposite, meaning we fail to see how our words and actions affect the emotions and feelings of others. What's the answer if there is one?

Thinking before we speak and being consciously aware of our words when we do speak is a good place to start. Understand what the person or people have gone through emotionally and in terms of action and consider pausing and waiting for them to speak first. There is absolute grace in pausing before we speak, before we act, and, yes, I get it—sometimes we must act quickly and speak quickly before being fully aware of what our actions might do or not do. Those are called crucial conversations; however, more times than not, there is time to hit the pause button and listen. Pretend that we have an imaginary red button by our finger, and when we feel the need to chime in and offer unsolicited advice, we lift our finger and hit the pause button instead. This is an act of grace.

The Metaphysical Approach

Before things of a metaphysical nature were written about, there was finger pointing and accusations of being connected to the 'devil'. Nobody talked about subjects such as tarot, mediumship, psychic abilities, clairvoyance, etc., until, that is, books were published on these subjects. The fascinating aspect lies in the evolution of metaphysics, a concept that means beyond the physical realm. If you visited one of the major book chains, you would find metaphysics in the "occult" section, surrounded by themes such as witches, warlocks, séances, and so on. Then metaphysics became more mainstream with the increased visibility of mediumship and psychic gifts. Unsure of what to call it next, it began to take on a more New Age feel, incorporating concepts such as ascended masters, astrology, numerology, and other related subjects.

As inspirational stories of people experiencing healing through these gifts emerged, the category became known as New Age. As people began to associate this newfound spirituality with a religion, a New Age religion emerged. Unity churches not only embrace these gifts, but they also mention and discuss Jesus, God, and the Archangels.

Now it has accelerated to the point where it cannot be denied that people's lives have been changed, so now the category has been adjusted to Self-Transformation. People are awakening to the new age of self-transformation, where metaphysical gifts are useful, helpful, and healing. This new age is what the shift in consciousness is all about, which I describe in another chapter in this book.

Metaphysical gifts are God-given gifts that everyone possesses. These gifts manifest themselves in different ways to help us in times of darkness. The purpose of readings is not to provide us with answers, but to offer us clarity, comfort, and closure. Only the creator knows the future for certain; reading provides glimpses, which is all we can hope for. This is not an exclusive club, but a sacred calling to those with an open mind. All we need to do is place our hand on the doorknob that opens an inner door leading to that space filled with mystery, questions, curiosity, unanswered questions, and intrigue. Anyone can do this, but we will never know if we don't try.

CHAPTER EIGHT

NAVIGATION

"Destiny is not fate, it's navigation."

—Richie Norton

OVERVIEW

This chapter is about navigating everyday subjects such as forgiveness and intentions, as well as challenging ones like transformation, victimhood, setting boundaries, and the very difficult subject of suicide. The Universe will provide soft landings for us all. This final chapter involves navigating difficult areas of our lives to find our mission and purpose in life that will take us to our destiny.

Forest of Forgiveness

"I can forgive, but I can't forget." All of us at one time or another have been hurt and have uttered that statement. So, we embark on a path to find it within ourselves to forgive the person or people who did us wrong. Forgiving someone is one thing, but forgetting about it is another matter. Trying to forgive someone is difficult, but forgetting about it seems to be a near impossibility. How do we go about doing this forgiving but not forgetting? It's not one of those situations where it looks easy on paper but not easy to do. This is one of those situations where it doesn't look good on paper for a reason. You must be able to compartmentalize to separate the two, and that's no small task. And how about being forgiven? Let's imagine that there is a Forest of Forgiveness where we can go and figure this forgiveness thing out.

First, notice the quietness in the forest. Perfect time to go deep inside our thoughts. Second, look at the way we asked for their forgiveness; did we in fact ask for their forgiveness or just assume that it would be freely given to us? That would be a pivotal starting point in the forest. Third, find the people in the forest that we have hurt and ask for forgiveness, whether they grant it to us or not. These people are not hard to find because they are hiding in plain sight. Fourth, forgiveness is a two-way street.... asking for and at the same time giving forgiveness. One cannot exist without the other.

Offering forgiveness is a first step to living a life of grace. To admit that we were wrong is to surrender to a higher calling.

How did the people we sought forgiveness from respond? There will always be someone who responds in a positive manner. That's good behavior to emulate. There are also people who will decline our offer, and that's okay too. We're called to give them the gift of forgiveness, and it's up to them to accept it. Everyone has their path of acceptance, and we should never question what that path looks like.

We also need to cleanse our minds of negative thoughts about those that have done us wrong. Notice that I did not say "clear" our minds but cleanse our minds. After cleansing, something is lighter, cleaner, purer, and more energetic. It just doesn't have the same properties as it used to.

"Cleanse my thoughts about the people that I need to forgive. Cleanse my fears surrounding forgiving myself. Cleanse my doubts about my intentions."

Back in the forest, as it's starting to rain. A soft mist starts to fall. Rain not only cleanses the forest but also allows growth to occur. We need cleansing as well so we can help nurture our forgiveness path for others. Visualize walking in the forest, walking towards the mist, knowing that the Creator loves us unconditionally and forgives us unconditionally. Stop for a moment and give thanks to the heavens for whence the cleansing came from.

Self-Transformation

What is the most difficult journey? Some may point to trying to "find yourself" in this world that we live in that seems to border on the surreal. Check this out.

The journey from "Who am I?" to "Who I am" is a shift in consciousness.

When we go from a question to a statement, we embark on the real journey of self-transformation. When we begin to accept who we are, faults and all, and slowly, but steadily, take on an inner form that finally feels like we've arrived into a new set of skin, which makes us strangely comfortable. Granted, this self-transformation can and normally does take a long time, maybe even a majority of a lifetime, to get to a place where we're comfortable with our self-transformation.

How do we arrive at this place of who we really are as citizens of the Universe? Here's a suggestion: Every New Year's Day—or more often if you like—ask yourself two questions: 1) Who am I at this point in my life? 2) How am I progressing towards living the life I desire? There's no need to take a lot of notes, except for mental ones. The closer you get to the core of knowing who you are, the closer you are to arriving in a new sort of comfortable clothes.

When we arrive at the place where we like ourselves, then the transformation starts.

This is the true evolution that our soul has been waiting for. When we learn to accept the natural beauty of our qualities that make us uniquely gifted in this world, then the rest of our universe opens. If you're going to ask other people their input on how you are as a person, that's going to border on energy that is wasted. You need to provide your own input. This realization that you can confidently say to yourself, "Here is what I am," is true growth. Stand tall.

Into the Mist

There are times in our lives when we must leave the warm and cozy energy environment of our sanctuary and walk in the footprints of our ancestors and follow the pathways of where our Higher Self wants us to go. The Higher Self is neither a false nor true self, since those concepts are philosophical in nature and in no way connected to the metaphysical self, which is the Higher Self.

The Higher Self is the point of contact with God.

It's a thirty-thousand-foot view of everything; it communicates with our soul, our intuition, and our guides. When we feel that urge to go in a different direction, it's the Higher Self that is guiding the ship. The Higher Self is not encased in any part of our physical body, but it is entwined and intersects with our consciousness.

When we feel the urge to do something or "leave the nest," the Higher Self likes to gently guide us as if we were walking into the mist. The image we should take with us, walking into the mist. With the energy of our Higher Self, the mist will take us into new chapters of our lives if we allow it. Trust your Higher Self. It will lead you in and out of the mist to new discoveries about your path and yourself.

When we start to feel as if we're in a mist or fog, it means a shift of the highest order. Could it be that this "uneasy" feeling, this shift, is an awakening to a new and better us? There is a higher purpose at this point in our lives. Only by going in the mist will we ever find out.

Valley of Victimhood

These days, there is much to be concerned and depressed about. Politics, war, famine, and so on—if we could turn the clock back 50, 60 years (or even longer) ago, we would discover that nothing much has changed. In fact, we could turn the clock back so far that we would be using a sundial. Atrocities against humanity, such as discrimination, crime, poverty, abuse, racism, murder, and torture, give us significant cause for concern, particularly in relation to individuals and situations that require prayers, love, positive energy, and support, particularly in terms of resources.

These people fall into the valley of victims and never recover. These are the people that we should spare no expense for when it comes to offering help. We cannot run fast enough into this valley to help those who truly need it. However, there is a danger looming over the horizon... something is in our way, and that something is a group of people planting their flag of "Look at me, I'm a victim... everyone else, take a number." Into the valley they go, staking their claims of victimhood and preventing us from using our time and resources to help those who really need it, like the scenarios mentioned above. This is because they are offended, which may not make them a victim. Along the way, we all get offended, sometimes more than others, but that doesn't make us victims.

True victims like the ones mentioned above need us now more than ever to help them get out of the valley. While we're at it, we need to send positive energy to those who have been offended so they can move on with their lives. We have an obligation to help everybody, anyway we can, and even if it is just to let them know we're here and we love them. The folks that are offended also need love too because maybe underneath that layer of offense is a pit of despair. It is our calling from the Universe to make this world and beyond a place of higher energy and vibrations by impacting the life of one soul at a time. Most of the time, we just need someone to break our fall as we tumble into the valley. To those who have been offended, I once heard a great line to open a conversation. (Thank you, S.L.) "Help me understand." This line is very effective at communicating mutual lines of agreement. Perhaps we can offer this up: "Help me understand why you are offended." The answer might surprise us.

The Grace of Intentions

We've heard it all before regarding someone having good intentions, but things didn't turn out like anyone expected, meaning the desired outcome wasn't reached. "Well, he/she/they had good intentions, but…" Then comes the litany of where the person or persons made mistakes. Comments such as "They should have known better," "What a mess they made," "Now it's worse," "Why did they have to interfere?" And my favorite one, "Why didn't they leave it well enough alone?"

What started out as a sincere compliment somehow got hijacked and has turned into stinging criticism of an individual or group who were only trying to help. Well-intentioned people hear about it repeatedly from various sources about how they failed when all they were doing was trying to help a person or situation where nobody else was going to step up.

Good, well-meaning intentions are blessed by the Universe.

Somebody tries to help someone in distress as onlookers are doing what they do best… looking on. Your intuition will lead you in the right direction as the cup of grace will be full. Why do we have to add "but" every time when a simple "well, it didn't work out, but their intentions were good (or pure)"?

Yes, sometimes things are not going to go well when we feel an urge to help, but by listening to our intuition and our Higher Self, we go by the grace of God to offer help. Shouldn't their actions be applauded and not criticized?

Let's make our intentions a path for others to follow.

Let's go into the mind of someone who has tried to help, and it didn't work out. I wonder if they're thinking, "Well, that's the last time I get involved." What about the people who heard about this or saw it happen? After observing or hearing what happened, how quickly will they offer help in the future?

There are people in this world who are just looking for a hand to help them, even if it's the simplest of things that may look on the outside like a small task, but to them is the break they were looking for to give them hope that someone cares.

Next time when we see someone that needs a helping hand, use that gut feeling to help you decide, no matter how small the act, to help, especially knowing that grace will be in the act itself. When it comes to us, let's not forget there's a flip side to the coin of intentions. For those who reach out and offer help to us, let us acknowledge them and forget about the "but" and simply offer thanks for helping. It doesn't matter if your hand is clean or dirty or whether you offer your right or left hand… to those that are in need, they aren't too picky.

The Suicide Survivors Club

A pandemic that has existed for decades and is spreading, unfortunately, is the suicide rate. According to world-wide statistics, more than 700,000 people annually take their lives. We hope and pray that these wounded souls find peace in the afterlife. It is my belief that they do not languish forever in the bowels of hell, even though I do believe that such a place exists but maybe not by that name.

There are many explanations and theories as to why family members, friends, and co-workers are here one day and then vanish the next day, never to be seen again in this lifetime. Some of us understood because we sensed something was wrong, while the rest of us never saw it coming. No signs, no warnings, nothing remaining except memories and lots of questions.

So, what happens to the loved ones that are left behind? They are left holding the baggage of the departed.

What happened? Where did we fail them? What did we do? What did we say? Why is this happening to us? How are we going to explain this to people in the outside world? We feel embarrassed, ashamed, at a loss for words, and guilty because we hate them for what they did, and most importantly, we feel alone because a big part of us died along with them.

This is the suicide survivors club because they also experience death. Maybe not permanent death, but one could argue that the loved ones left behind experience death every day as they relive that horrible, devastating day when they experienced the news. This is a "club" that nobody wants to belong to. I call it a club because they share a common grief that very few people on the outside can understand or relate to.

What can we do to support them? One thing might be not to ask them how they're doing. The response may come back, "I'm doing ok." This is because few are good at asking for help. Another thing to consider not asking is, "What can I do to help?" We are not good at telling people how they can help. At some point it's okay to ask the above questions, but here are some other ways we can help.

SPACE—In the beginning we can let them know that we are going to be reaching out in the coming days (2-3 days), but for now we are going to give them a little space.

This one you might have to play it by ear, as I know some people insist on being there to support them, and that's ok, but what I'm hearing (from the Universe) is that not everyone wants to be surrounded by loved ones at that point. They need some time in the beginning to sit by themselves and reflect on what has happened. It's hard to hear our inner voice when there are outside voices around us.

ACTION—Time to act and plan a lunch or dinner. Let's not ask them if they want to go because they may feel like it's an imposition to accept. Make a reservation and tell them the plans. They may feel guilty for refusing the invitation because of the trouble that was involved in making the reservations, so hopefully they will accept. The above action will depend on a couple of things: make the action gentle and accept the fact that they still might say no. Our actions might be the first step for someone else to finish the invitation.

CONVERSATION—Asking questions is fine, but a conversation will engage them more. We all tend to ask closed-ended questions... questions that can only be answered with a yes or no. Open-ended questions cannot be answered with a yes or no but instead start a conversation.

I worked with a sales consultant who we will refer to as S.L. His opening line was, "Help me understand." This is a terrific line. Example: days after someone has lost a loved one and taken their own life… "Help me understand what the past few days have been like for you." "I cannot imagine what you're going through." You get the idea.

These conversations will last a lifetime as we must continue to reach out in the coming days, weeks, months, and years. If we're going to be lifelong friends, then the healing is lifelong.

All clubs have dues, but members in this club have paid their dues and then some. Let's not be a spectator to their grief but participate by doing all we can to help heal their pain.

Borders, Boundaries, Sanctuaries

Looking at the heading above, what thoughts run through our minds when it comes to the words borders, boundaries, and sanctuaries? Looking at the definition may help us understand the differences. I took liberties with the definitions to make it simple (for me).

BORDERS—On the edge of a boundary or flat surface.

BOUNDARY—A line that marks the limits of an area or a dividing line.

SANCTUARY—A place of refuge or safety.

At times in our lives, we need all three, sometimes all at once. For example: We set up a boundary for someone who keeps invading our space without our permission. Boundaries either keep people in or out. There is no crossing a boundary. It is set in stone, or at least that is the idea. But they keep coming and coming, breaking through the boundaries despite our objections to slow down or stop, and they realize the borders are just ahead, knowing that this will be easy to overcome and now the only thing left is our sanctuary. One of two things have happened: either they did not understand or catch on to the signals, or they just do not care.

This can happen during conversations, physical confrontations (God forbid), family meetings (again, God forbid), or any situation that involves contact with another human being. It does not matter about the order if we recognize these areas of engagement. Many of us may put the border first as a softer way of sending signals, then when they keep invading our space, we set the boundaries as a way of saying, "No more."

Our space is sacred; it is ours and no one else's.

The sanctuary is where we feel safe. We may not own or have much in possessions, but we have our own space. Cherish it, protect it, and let the Universe speak to us. Let's choose our sanctuary of sacred space wisely, for it will serve us well.

Peace

About Jerry

Jerry is a clairvoyant medium with certifications in mediumship, psychic mediumship, spiritualism, natural law, remote viewing, and clairvoyance. He studied mediumship at Arthur Findlay College in England and has a BA in Metaphysical Science. He will obtain his MA in 2024 and his doctorate in 2025.

Jerry has a masters in Metaphysical & Humanistic Sciences and is currently studying for his doctoral.

Jerry is of Scottish descent as a member of the MacDonald Clan Ranald and is a direct descendant of John Wallace, who fought alongside his brother William Wallace for Scotland's independence. Jerry lives in Florida with his wife Mary and his three children, Katie, Patrick, and Andrew, and his three grandchildren, Quinn, Kellan, and Kelly.

BOOKS FROM JERRY MCDANIEL

CHANNELING the MOTHERSHIP
Messages from the Universe
Published 2017

BEYOND THE RATIONAL REALM
Lifting the Veil of the Spirit World
Published 2020

Books available at online retailers and select metaphysical shops and bookstores. Also available on my website, www.jmacmedium.com

Made in the USA
Columbia, SC
03 September 2025

91855704-9642-4a78-b78e-585d9ac6c33aR01